PRAYERS
for Our
COUNTRY

Daily
Prayer Book

 Publications International, Ltd.

Contributing Writers: Ann Broyles, Christine A. Dallman, June Eaton, Marie D. Jones, Crystal Kirgiss, Susan J. Letham, Christopher Lyon, Wallis C. Metts, Jr., Ph.D., Jennifer John Ouellette, and Carol Stigger.

Quotations compiled by Joan Loshek.

Photo Credits: Thomas Franklin/Bergen Record/Corbis Saba; Index Stock Imagery: Sandra Baker; Erin Garvey; Mark Gibson; Henryk Kaiser; **James P. Rowan Photography; Laurence Parent Photography, Inc.; Nik Wheeler Photography; Paul Rezendes Photography; Robert Holmes Photography:** Robert Holmes; Brian McGilloway; **Stone/Getty Images:** Rob Boudreau; Dennis O'Clair; **SuperStock:** James L. Amos; Scott Barrow; Ron Dahlquist; Emmanuel Faure; Gala; Richard Heinzen; Kent & Charlene Krone; Roger Allyn Lee; Jean-Pierre Lescourret; David W. Middleton; Mark Newman; Peter Van Rhijn; Steve Vidler; John Warden; **Tom Bean Photography; William B. Folsom Photography, Inc.**

Prayers for Our Country

We all need prayer. As individuals, as families, as communities, and as a country. Whether they are prayers of praise or pleading, our prayers must be lifted up so they can be heard. And as people of God, we know that anything we have to say—no matter how simple or how grand—will be heard.

Praying is a sign of hope, for us personally and for our country. We pray because of the strength of our faith in God. Our prayers are evidence of our faith that God will respond. This response is God's way of proving his love for us.

This book of daily prayers has been designed as a tool for talking with God. It includes many prayers for our country. Some days feature prayers of thanksgiving; other days offer requests for God's guidance for our country's leaders and its people; and still others lead you to praise God for his grace, mercy, and creative genius.

Make these prayers your own as you talk with God. Deepen your relationship with God; bask in his power and love.

January 1
New Year's Day

God, as we start a new year, remind us of all we have to be proud of in America. We are proud of our cities, our farms, our schools, our hospitals, our government, our natural wonders, our monuments, our history, our discoveries, our knowledge, our creativity, and our vision. But mostly, we are proud of our people—individuals from all walks of life and from all ethnic traditions. Our people, more than anything else, define who we are. Help us to act and speak in ways that make us all proud to be Americans. Our strength is our people. Amen.

January 2

Wondrous Creator, you carved out the Grand Canyon in its immensity and etched the details of the Blue Ridge Mountains. Your power created Niagara Falls yet also brought into being the tiniest fish in the Chesapeake Bay. From your imagination came Yosemite, the Great Lakes, Maine's rugged coast, the Everglades, Crater Lake. Your fingers fashioned sequoias and redwoods, lilies and jasmine, cardinals and great blue herons. As we appreciate the incredible natural beauty of this great nation, help us to see your handiwork in it and to find inspiration so we can create beauty in our own lives and world. In your creative power, we pray. Amen.

January 3

Dear Lord, help us to understand the hatred in our world. Please guide us to a more peaceful life. As Americans we live free from constraints on our lives and free to make our own decisions. Help us to help others achieve the same.

☆ ☆ ☆ ☆ ☆

Liberty is the soul's right to breathe.

Henry Ward Beecher, *Life Thoughts*

January 4

A new year is upon this dear country of ours, God. When I reflect on the unpredictability of national events, it's a poignant reminder to place my trust in you and to thank you for each precious day of life in our free America. Go with us into this year, with your light of truth and your gentle grace to lead and guide us on a path of peace that, in time, may reach the whole world. In your name, amen.

★ ★ ★ ★ ☆

What is the American Dream? For Americans,
it is anything we want it to be.

January 5

Lord God, when I feel my security shaken, when I wonder what will come next in the events of this great nation, help me keep my eyes on you, to trust in you. You have promised to be strong for all who run to you. You are a shelter in uncertainty, an immovable rock of security in an insecure world. Thank you that your eternal kingdom will never fail. And as I place my faith in you, I can then pray for my beloved country with a renewed sense of calm, knowing that you will never leave me nor forsake me. Amen.

January 6

God bless us one and all. God bless the men and women who lost their lives this past year; bless their families also. God bless all the courageous workers across the nation, including those who kept the peace, fought the fires, taught the children, wrote the books, healed the sick, and sang the songs of our nation's joys and sorrows. God bless the children, the husbands and wives, the sisters and brothers, the neighbors and friends. God bless the brokenhearted and the diminished in spirit, the grieving and the fearful. God bless us one and all.

☆　☆　☆　☆　☆

They say you can tell what something is worth by how much a buyer is willing to pay. By that measure, what is freedom worth?

January 7

Loving Lord, guide us, your people, to act righteously in times of trouble. Guard our thoughts and our lips. Banish hate and bigotry from our minds, and teach us how we can live together in peace.

You are our strength, Father. Give us the courage to keep our spirits high, even when we are feeling low, and to pour out our tenderness on others and bring light to the darkness, all in your name.

☆ ☆ ☆ ☆ ☆

Great leaders may be born and not made. But they can only be elected if good people vote for them.

January 8

God,
Thank you for your strength.
Thank you for your love.
Thank you for your guidance.
Thank you for your patience.
Thank you for your wisdom.
Thank you for your creation.
Thank you for your joy.
Thank you for your power.
Thank you for your majesty.

Thank you for giving us a land in which we are free to thank
you, worship you, and honor you.
Amen.

January 9

Lord, you measure out to each of us the sum of our days, each
one unique and perfect in its way. Help us honor your gift by
living each day of our lives to the fullest, as you intended.
If we can help someone today, let us do it and not put it off
until tomorrow.
If we can speak a kind word today, let us do it and not put it
off until tomorrow.
If we can praise someone today, let us do it and not put it off
until tomorrow.
If we can love someone today, let us do it and not put it off
until tomorrow.
If we can offer thanks today, let us do it and not put it off until
tomorrow.
You are the perfect giver. Help us be thankful recipients of
your bounty.

January 10

Be with me, O God.

Be with my family, friends, and neighbors.

Be with those who live in my city or town
   and with all who reside in my state.

Be with all the citizens of these United States,
   and so bind us together that we know ourselves to be
   united,

   connected,

   as one.

Let us feel your presence.

Hear us lift our unique voices as one voice,
   praising you,

   giving thanks,

   offering our lives to your service.

Be with me, O God, now and always. Amen.

January 11

Please Lord, help me to be strong. Give me patience and strength. I pray the same prayer for my country, Lord.

Let us be just and reasonable, and give us wisdom. I am your child, and we are your nation. May we all make you proud today and every day. Amen.

★ ★ ★ ★ ★

Beneath the touch of a helping hand, we can feel God's strong grasp. If we hold on, we are no longer alone.

January 12

God of Peace, violence is everywhere. It is the weapon of evil. We never know when it will erupt, even in ourselves, and we are unprepared when it does.

You have seen violence among your people since the days of Eden. You alone know how to confront and combat it.

Father, we seek your wisdom. Teach us how to conduct ourselves in the face of violence. Help us as we try to understand senseless acts that hurt and kill. Preserve us wherever evil threatens to strike.

Help us confront the problem of violence with courage, reason, and compassion. You have promised peace to those who love you. Make us willing servants in the struggle for an end to violence and the beginning of a peaceful coexistence.

January 13

In this quiet, cold season we turn our hearts toward you, O Lord. May our hearts be as open and bare toward you as the winter trees are in the skyline. Let nothing come between us— no pretense, no excuses, no barriers of any kind. In our bareness may we dare to be real, to show our true selves, and to trust that you love us no matter what. In your great love we pray, amen.

☆ ☆ ☆ ☆ ☆

Know the benediction of the Lord in these days! In all your comings and goings, know that he is there. In all your joys and triumphs, know that he upholds you. In all your worries and heartaches, know that he cares. And in all your worship, celebrating, dancing, laughing—wherever you are—know that he is pleased.

January 14

Often, Lord, fear runs rampant through my mind. I'm afraid for my country, I'm afraid for my family, and I'm afraid for victims of cruel acts. Most of my fears are unfounded, Lord. I know that. You have promised to be with me, and I need to trust your presence in my life. Please help me, and others, to live by your word and in peace.

★ ★ ★ ★ ★

We know that there is no greater burden than to think no one cares or understands. That is why the promise of your presence is so precious to us, you who said: "Remember, I am with you always, to the end of the age."

January 15
Martin Luther King, Jr.'s Birthday

Martin lived among us, O God, and showed us how to live in love. He preached, taught, and marched in the name of love. He was thrown into a jail cell yet spoke only love in return. When he and his family endured bomb threats and verbal abuse, he responded in love. He was shot down because some who heard him could not accept his message of love. Yet the events his words set in motion could not be stopped, and our world has not been the same since Dr. King led the way.

Help us to remember his dream, O Lord, that one day all people can dwell together in unity regardless of their differences. Give us the courage to act in love, speak in love, respond only out of love—not just today as we honor Dr. King, but all days, so that the world can still learn that love and tolerance are the only way to live in freedom as one United States. In the spirit of that great love that can unite us, we pray. Amen.

January 16

The opportunity to dream, to chase my dreams, to realize my dreams is part of the privilege of being an American. I thank you for that privilege, Father. Help me never stop dreaming, never stop reaching, never give up hope. Be my strength, my stamina, my victory, Lord. And be honored in my quest for excellence in all that I do. Amen.

★ ★ ★ ★ ★

It is not a color that makes an American. It is not a religion that makes an American. It is simply a belief—"I am American, and I am proud."

January 17

God of our mothers and fathers, since the beginning of time
you have been a constant presence in the life of humanity. You
have watched over us as we have explored new lands, conquered
other civilizations, waged wars, and searched for peace.
Through your gift of creativity we have written great literature,
made medical advances, created instruments of destruction,
and become reliant on technology. As our empires have risen
and fallen, you have quietly continued to offer us your great
gift of love—a gift the world so desperately needs right now.

Give us and our leaders the creativity needed to build our
nation. Fill us with your loving spirit that we might boldly
work to bring about a world of justice and peace for all people,
regardless of nationality. And may our efforts combine with
all your children everywhere, that the world might know peace.
Amen.

January 18

History reveals that few if any nations have ever enjoyed so much freedom, in all levels of society, as we do here in the United States of America. I move about so easily in the freedoms I enjoy, Father. Sometimes I forget that they're rare and wonderful gifts. Surely you mean for us to use our liberty to give something back and not just to take; to offer respect and love to our fellow citizens, not prejudice and strife; to act responsibly, not selfishly. Help us, Lord, by your grace, to enjoy and preserve our freedoms in the spirit of your love and righteousness. Amen.

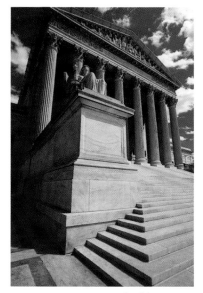

U.S. Supreme Court building

January 19

Lord, many of our country's heroes have been born on the battlefield, but heroes can emerge in any event of our nation's history. Today we give you thanks for the many ordinary men and women who have shown heroism in daily life.

You have taught us that to give ourselves for others—to love our neighbors—is the highest calling a person can answer. Those who give their lives and those who risk them to keep others safe deserve our highest praise and deepest gratitude.

Bless our heroes, Lord, both great and small. We are touched by their sacrifices and enriched by their example.

January 20

Thank you, Almighty God, Creator of Life, for giving me this day. It is a unique gift. Help me live by your word and give as well as receive. Lead me from trivial thoughts and ways, and lead me toward kind gestures and thoughtful deeds. Amen.

★ ★ ★ ★ ★

The difference between a dream and a reality is the action we take in-between.

January 21

God, we are a strong and mighty people. We fall, but we rise again. We fail, but we try again. We fight the good fight, and we do not give in to evil. We are blessed, and we are grateful for our blessings. We are compassionate and caring and kind. We are proud and bold and true. Thank you, God, for making us Americans.

★ ★ ★ ★ ☆

Justice is fairness and truth and reason—jumping into action to right a wrong.

January 22

What beautiful harmony exists within this diversified nation, God. Certainly, our differences are many, and sometimes our disagreements are heated, but we have not lost our sense of what unites us. We have found success in this great experiment of government by which many have been knit together by a common love for freedom. The world looks on in wonder, and sometimes I do, too. It's a miracle—a true miracle, Lord! Thank you for allowing me to experience it. I love being an American.

★ ★ ★ ★ ★

Freedom cannot be seen or touched or put in a box or marked on a map. It is not an object or a thing but a way of moving through the world unrestrained by the limitations, beliefs, or desires of others.

January 23

Sometimes life makes no sense. Bad things happen to good people, the weak and innocent suffer, and our world seems out of step with your plan. It's hard to raise our voices in song when our hearts are heavy with sadness. And it's hard to move on when each minute lasts an eternity. When doubt and confusion come calling, Lord, strengthen our faith, just for today.

Just for today, Lord, give us the strength to live in your name and do your will.

Just for today, Lord, remind us that everything has a place in your divine order and that our faith will be rewarded eternally.

Help us stay faithful as we walk with you in our hearts, just for today.

January 24

Rejoice, America! Shout from every rooftop, "We are the brave ones, the bold ones, the keepers of the light." Shout to the heavens, "We are the proud warriors for peace, the torch-bearers of truth and justice." Shout to the hills, "We are the generous and charitable, the kind and compassionate, the wise and understanding." Shout across the flatlands, "We are hope manifested in human form, love made real, freedom expressed." Shout over the oceans, "We are guardians of liberty and soldiers of righteousness." Rejoice, America!

★ ☆ ★ ☆ ☆

In these United States, all things are possible, all dreams are achievable, all goals are reachable. In these United States, every man, woman, and child is blessed with the freedom to be great and to do great things.

January 25

God, I am thankful today to live in the land of the free and the home of the brave. Unfortunately, it sometimes takes a trying time for people to pull together, but there is no spirit like the spirit of America! We are not run by one person alone but by the vote of all people. We do not turn people away because of their appearance, race, or religion. America is the home of self-sacrifice and fearless courage. Today, I implore you to bless America! Amen.

★　★　★　★　☆

To love one is to love all, for in truth we are all one. To know one is to know all, for in truth we are all the same inside. To help one is to help all, for in truth we are all interdependent. To give to one is to give to all, for in truth we are all connected.

January 26

I ask you to bless America, Lord God. Help her not to grow weary in doing what is right, no matter how difficult it may be to do so. Help me, as one of her citizens, to do my part today by choosing what is honest, what is true, what is kind, what is good, what is patient, what promotes peace, and what brings honor to the title I bear: proud American.

★ ★ ★ ★ ★

Let us, on the day set aside for this purpose, give thanks to the Ruler of the universe for the strength which He has vouchsafed us to carry on our daily labors and for the hope that lives within us of the coming of a day when peace and the productive activities of peace shall reign on every continent.

President Franklin D. Roosevelt, October 31, 1939

January 27

Compassionate God, our country has known great sorrow. We understand that pain and death are a part of life, but although the world is full of suffering, it is also full of healing—your healing, O God.

In our suffering, our nation always has chosen to unite and turn to you in prayer. We feel the pain of all your children: the poor and homeless, innocent victims of violence, survivors of natural disasters, those who have lost homes and belongings and livelihoods, those in physical pain.

Hear us, Lord, when we cry out to you. Bless us with your everlasting care. Bless us with your mercy, ease our pain, and restore us to wholeness. Only you can bring good out of evil and turn sorrow into joy.

January 28

Lord, help us to make the right choices when trouble enters our lives. We can choose to act from fear, or we can choose to respond from love.

Help us to go within and seek your view before we act. Lead us to peace within ourselves, and grant us your wisdom so we gain insight and respond from love and strength.

When trouble bursts uninvited into our lives, remind us who we are: children of God. Remind us that our pledge is to life, here and for all eternity. Teach us how to follow your example.

When sadness comes, Lord, walk with us. Open our eyes so we see how it makes us strong. It's through our trials that we grow to fully become who we are. Pray with us so we make the right choice. Fill us with the power of love.

January 29

Father, the flag is a symbol of the country I love. When her colors touch the sky, I get a tear in my eye. Old Glory is her nickname, and I pray that she will wave over this land for years to come. Let me never disgrace her, for she lauds the honor of brave people who died to keep her flying. And may my salutes be sincere and my pledges heartfelt, for she represents your gifts to me of life, liberty, and the pursuit of happiness. Amen.

★　★　★　★　☆

[The American flag] means the rising up of a valiant young people against an old tyranny, to establish the most momentous doctrine that the world has ever known, or has since known—the right of men to their own selves and to their liberties.

Henry Ward Beecher, May 1861

January 30

God of hope, help us to be a hopeful people.

When things don't go as we expect, give us optimism
    for the future.

When we feel discouraged, give us encouragement.

When all we can see is darkness around us, show us the light.

When times get rough, give us courage.

When we feel sorrow, let us also know joy.

In all things and at all times, let us know your spirit
    and feel your love.

Amen.

January 31

Lord, there is a time for joy and a time for sorrow. Never let us forget that the world goes on in joyful times and in sorrowful ones. When the crying is done, help us heal. When the sorrow is over, let us celebrate our joy in life.

When we are sad, dear God, let us lay our sadness at your altar. When we are joyful, let us sing our joy to you. Let us be a bright light in our world. Fill us with your spirit and your love. Let us do your work for the good of our families, friends, and communities.

Open our eyes so we can see what we have, in all its beauty. Bless us with understanding of your ways and the faith to place our trust in you. Thank you, dear God, for your everlasting presence.

February 1

Lord, as the wheel of the year turns, be with us as we contemplate the seasons of life, each with a beauty and purpose:

In the spring of our lives, let us grow and gain strength, knowledge, and experience, ready for the time when we will be in full bloom. When summer comes, let us fulfill your hopes by being all we can be. Let our light shine out.

When fall draws close, let us reap the fruits of our early years. Help us become wise guides. As winter approaches, let us enjoy the quiet years and find true joy in what we've accomplished. Make us ready to enter into your light.

Lord, help us live in harmony with the seasons of our lives, ever moving toward the goal of eternal life with you.

February 2

I marvel at the majesty of our countryside, God. America is not only home to the free and the brave but also to luscious green landscapes and snowcapped mountains. America is a gorgeous, inspirational, freedom-draped land. Let us keep her beautiful for all future generations. Amen.

★ ★ ★ ★ ★

When we believe in a power greater than ourselves, the entire universe moves to reveal the brilliant handiwork of a loving and creative master walking alongside us and guiding our way.

February 3

How wonderful are the works of your hands, O God. Nowhere can we more appreciate your wonder than in our country's magnificent national parks.

This nation has such wealth. In it lies the breathtaking beauty and untold treasure of Yellowstone, Glacier, Grand Canyon, Mesa Verde, Denali, Yosemite, and all our national parks. Sparkling lakes and cool streams, awesome forests, majestic mountains, ancient caves, centuries-old cliff dwellings, volcanic formations—all declare your glory.

Gratefully we applaud the foresight of those who have gone before us to preserve the riches of your earth.

In your goodness, Lord, you have given us these havens of rest. Through them, all creation sings your praises.

February 4

For our neighbors and friends who are sad and lonely,
    Lord, hear our prayers.
For families struggling with poverty,
    Lord, hear our prayers.
For children who feel unloved and abandoned,
    Lord, hear our prayers.
For the government officials who keep our nation united,
    Lord, hear our prayers.
For the religious leaders who guide our nation,
    Lord, hear our prayers.
For all our nation's citizens,
    Lord, hear our prayers.

February 5

Bless the leaders of the world, O God.

Give each leader the wisdom to see clearly,
    the presence of mind to consider all possibilities
      before acting,
    the compassion to see those who are hurting,
    the lack of ego that leads to cooperation,
    the humility to listen to others,
    the patience to talk things through,
    the courage to make tough decisions,
    the faith to trust in your power,
    and the strength to work for peace in all situations.

Bless those who lead and we who support their leadership. May the goal of peace be always foremost in all our minds. Amen.

February 6

Lord, we ask your healing for our nation. Grant us understanding so we can make good choices. Cast aside confusion, and help us see the truth of who we are. Bless our leaders; help them make decisions that preserve our peaceful way of life.

Lord, give us peace of mind. Make us compassionate, and help us see you in everyone. Bless our families: the heart of our nation. Love begins in the home and flows from there.

Lord, endow us with health. Draw us closer, and help us grow in faith. Bless the spirit of America: freedom, faith, and friendship. Help us make it a beacon of faith that shines into the world.

Grant us strength of spirit. This we ask for the good of our families, our country, and in your name, O God.

February 7

Father, help me embrace my responsibilities as a citizen of this land of many freedoms. Remind me that rights and responsibilities go hand in hand, that freedom cannot exist without careful and consistent stewardship of it. Keep me focused on the privileges I enjoy so that my burden of duty will seem light. And let me serve well, as unto you. In your name, amen.

★ ★ ★ ★ ☆

Today, I long to make a difference—to pass along peace and joy and somehow resurrect hope in weary hearts.

February 8

Blessed Parent, we are a strong and loving nation, but now we question our place in an ever-changing world. Please give to us a new perspective on who we are and what we must do to forever work for peace, for freedom, for prosperity for all the world's citizens. Help us to spread love where only fear walked before, that we might be a guiding light for all other nations to look to for hope and understanding. Amen.

☆　☆　☆　☆　☆

*It is my living sentiment, and by the blessing of God
it shall be my dying sentiment—Independence
now and Independence forever!*

President John Adams, days before his death, July 1, 1826

February 9

Dear God, how can we leave America better for our children and grandchildren? How can we make sure we leave them with an inheritance that is not sealed with war, hunger, and terror? Please, Lord, help us build a stronger foundation for our country. Let us build upon the morals, ethics, and values of those who came before us to sustain generations to come. Please help us build and maintain friendships here and abroad that will support our children. Amen.

★ ★ ★ ★ ☆

Faith, as sturdy as the stone foundation beneath a century-old house, forms the bedrock upon which I stand, unswayed despite the winds of change.

February 10

Lord, when we lay our impossible tasks and challenges at your feet, we soon find they are not obstacles to you.

In these times, problems sometimes loom large and seem to have no solution. But you have given your people a determined spirit, born of the courage you have inspired in us. We have faith that you will show us the way to overcome even the most overwhelming barriers.

In joy and thanksgiving we surrender our deepest concerns and anxieties to you, Lord, knowing you can conquer all.

February 11

Let me be a light, dear Lord, that shines in dark corners. Let me be a beacon of hope and a friend to all in need. Let me be part of the solution and not part of the problem. Let me help and never hinder. Let me serve and ask for nothing in return. Let me heal the wounds of those who suffer. Let me offer support to those who grieve. Let me be a light, dear Lord, that shines in dark corners.

☆ ☆ ☆ ☆ ☆

When the darkness casts shadows upon us
and the answers are nowhere in sight,
hope lifts us up on a wing and a prayer
and carries us back to the light.

February 12
Lincoln's Birthday

Some great men have led our nation, Father. Thank you for George Washington, our first president, and for Abraham Lincoln, a man of tremendous moral courage who helped lead us through our darkest days. Thank you for the succession of presidents who have helped us recover from the many and varied crises that have arisen along our way.

Help our current president, Father, as he navigates the many issues—national and global—that meet him daily. Grant him wisdom and foresight. Grant him courage and strength of character to do what is right. Help me to remember to pray for him because without your guidance and empowerment, Lord, the task is too big for him. But with you upholding him, he will do well. Amen.

Lincoln Memorial

February 13

Lord, I ask for strength today. I need strength to carry on with everyday tasks and guidance to perform them well. I often feel as though the pressure on me is so high that I will never be able to complete my day to your liking. Help me remember, God, that you will not give me anything I cannot handle. Help me live today to the best of my ability. Amen.

☆ ☆ ☆ ☆ ☆

People of hope ascend hills and mountains others have declared impossible to climb.

February 14

This month in which we celebrate love points to you, Father God. Thank you for showing us what love is and for placing within us the capacity to love. When I think of the innumerable ways we find, here in the United States, to express our love for each other, it warms my heart. I have to smile at the dozens of people standing around the greeting-card racks, shopping in earnest for just the right way to say "I love you" on Valentine's Day. Enlarge our love for one another this year to include not only those in our most intimate circles but also those who share our love for America, our home sweet home.

February 15

What a vast array of beauty this nation boasts! Your creativity, God, is evident east to west, north to south, in mountains, deserts, lakes, rivers, waterfalls, valleys, plains, prairies, and oceans. Those who live here also enjoy the benefits of abundant resources and rich agriculture. How fortunate we are to experience the blessings this awesome landscape affords. America the beautiful, America the bountiful! We praise you, Father, for creating such a place as this. Amen.

☆ ☆ ☆ ☆ ☆

We lack many things, but we possess the most precious of all—liberty!

President James Monroe, 1795

February 16

Father, right now in this country many are cold, hungry, in desperate need. Maybe they were born into poverty. Maybe a family crumbled, leaving them on the edge of survival. Maybe illness stole their resources. I know there have always been poor and needy people. I know there probably always will be. But I'm asking that you'll comfort those people in our country tonight.

Please bring hope to their hearts, food for their stomachs, and a decent place to sleep. Please help them to overcome the addictions and abuse that keep them so far from stability. Please bring loving people into their lives who will offer kindness and encouragement. Father, I ask that you will make this country stronger by strengthening the weakest among us. Thank you for offering your love to each of them.

February 17

Keep us united, Lord! Political issues can polarize us. Cultural differences can make us suspicious of one another. Our views on values can cause us to devalue those who don't agree with us. Please help us, God! Help us not to give in to hatred and abuse of one another. Help us rise above such base human tendencies and find the higher ground of tolerance, understanding, cooperation, respect, and, most of all, love. You said love was the greatest virtue. Let love have first place in our dealings with one another. In your name, amen.

February 18

In times of uncertainty, it is crucial to have someone by your side, someone to talk to, someone to lend support. Thank you, God, for always being there for our nation, for its leaders, and for each citizen of this great country. Amen.

☆ ☆ ☆ ☆ ☆

In every human breast, God has implanted a principle, which we call love of freedom; it is impatient of oppression and pants for deliverance.

Phillis Wheatley, American poet

February 19

We had feared so many of our fellow citizens had abandoned you, Lord, to go off on their own like wayward children forsaking their roots. But it takes just one taste of catastrophe, and they are back in your house, runaways returned to their safe nests.

You knew they would come back, Lord—that they couldn't make it on their own. Your children gather in churches and synagogues and mosques, seeking haven—seeking comfort. They stand together. They give each other courage, and they pray for peace.

Your house of worship is a place of refuge. It is a place of acceptance and comfort. How good it is to hear neighbors say again, "Let us go to the house of the Lord!" (Psalm 122:1), and you welcome them back. Thank you, Lord.

February 20

Heavenly Father, bless those who cry out for peace in times of war. Bless those who speak of love in times of hate. Bless those who move with courage in times of fear. Bless those who stand for justice in times of retribution. Bless those who keep the faith in times of uncertainty. Bless those who seek out good in times of evil. Bless those who believe in life in times of death.

☆ ☆ ☆ ☆ ☆

Faith is the still, small voice within that whispers,
"We shall overcome."
Hope is the gentle urging of the soul
to keep moving toward the light.
Charity is the quiet prompting of the spirit
to give of itself to those in need.
Love is the sweet song of the heart that rises like a bird on the wing.

February 21

Our children are fortunate. They wake with freedoms other children may never know. They are given an education and have their choice of what to eat for breakfast and what clothes to wear to school. They are given the right to express their thoughts and disagreements just as adult Americans can. They are not aware of the life some other children face. God, please protect America's children, and help us let them know how lucky they are to be Americans. Amen.

★　★　★　★　☆

Liberty, when it begins to take root, is a plant of rapid growth.

President George Washington, in a letter to James Madison, March 2, 1788

February 22
Washington's Birthday

God Almighty, creator of heaven and earth, please help Americans hold the memory of their great leaders of the past close to their hearts today and every day. Today is the birthday of our first commander in chief, the first president of this power-

ful nation. I praise the hard work and dedication of all those who walked this country before me. If it were not for them, life would not be as we know it now. May you continue to bless this nation, God, with strong, self-sacrificing leaders. Amen.

Washington Monument

February 23

Have mercy on our nation, Father! We are far from perfect, but we have not forgotten you and how you have brought us along from our earliest days. Forgive us for the ways in which we have departed from the right and the good. Open our hearts to the facets of your own character that you also desire for us as a nation: truth, honesty, integrity, compassion, justice, self-sacrifice, love. To the degree that we have abandoned these national virtues, Father, pardon us, we pray. Help us return to them and find the true source of our strength: the right and the good, rooted in your love. Amen.

February 24

(Based on Psalm 90)

Lord, you have been our dwelling place in all generations.

Before the earth was formed you were God.

In you there is no beginning or end.

You see earth's history in the blink of an eye.

You understand everything.

We live but for a moment yet act like we know everything.

Give us wisdom that we might put what we know

    into perspective.

Help us rise each morning with joy in our hearts.

Show us your great works.

Shine your glory on us.

Bless us and all that we do.

Amen.

February 25

Lord God, this nation is strong: strong emotionally, strong economically, strong spiritually. Show us how to use our many strengths to bring hope, relief, and dignity to struggling nations. Grant us compassion and generosity on a corporate level, as well as individually. In your name, amen.

☆ ☆ ☆ ☆ ☆

Liberty is the most contagious force in the world. It will eventually abide everywhere. No people of any race will remain slaves.

Earl Warren,
Chief Justice of the United States (1953–1969)

February 26

Dear God, you've blessed this nation from the beginning. You blessed us with courageous people who stood up for the idea of freedom. You blessed us with their foundational documents—the Declaration of Independence, the Constitution, the Bill of Rights—to keep us on the path of freedom. And you blessed us with their children, who held fast to the purpose of freedom.

Thank you, Father, for those beginnings. Help us to never forget them or take them for granted. Help us to hold on to our ideals, to cherish them, and to fight for them. Help us to never give them up, either to sudden onslaught or incremental compromise. Help us to always remember we were born to freedom and to never surrender it.

February 27

God, help our country emerge from the rubble of hard times with our heads held high. Help us keep faith in ourselves, our country, and in you, God. It's often difficult to see the sunshine through the storm. Please help us to see the compassion and profound strength we Americans share. Show us that Americans truly have the most giving spirit. Amen.

☆ ☆ ☆ ☆ ☆

The hopeful have a peace about them, a way of looking at everything that happens as an opportunity for growth and happiness. Their lives are not any easier than anyone else's; it's their attitude that sets them apart.

February 28

Father, be with our military personnel today. Encourage these special men and women who are serving our country in the Armed Forces. From generals to G.I.s, Lord, I ask that you would grant courage, honor, and integrity as each stands to protect and represent our beloved America. As a nation, we pray for their safety whether at home or abroad. And we pray for peace to prevail so that blood will not need to be shed. We pray this in your strong name. Amen.

★ ★ ★ ★ ☆

The blood of the American patriots is the seed of the nation's liberty. May we forever reap the fruit of their sacrifice in reverence and gratitude.

February 29

Pray for our nation, that it may remain strong and free. Pray for our people, that they may remain brave and true. Pray for our heritage, that it may shine as a light of possibility to other countries struggling with oppression. Pray for our environment, that it may be life-giving to the generations that follow. Pray for our spirit, that it may be steadfast and united from sea to shining sea.

★ ★ ★ ★ ☆

Sing the anthem, say the pledge, fly the flag:
Be proud to be American.

March 1

The month of March is here! We are moving forward into this year, Lord God, marching together as a nation. Renew our resolution to remain strong and united in purpose. As we discuss and debate our ideas about the best path to take, protect us from pride and prejudice. Make us circumspect and careful, decisive and fearless as we lead in the pursuit

of liberty. In humble submission to your wisdom and guidance, we pray. Amen.

March 2

Lord, when the time comes to make changes in our lives, help us accept them and know that they're for our good and our growth. Please God, let us, as a nation, make the same prayer for our country.

Make us willing to listen prayerfully for the quiet voice of divine discontent with which you speak to us. Give us the wisdom to hear and heed your words. We are creatures of habit; it is hard for us to move outside our comfort zones. But we know the voice of change ignored will get louder and louder, until it drowns out every other sound in our lives.

Endow us with courage, Lord, to listen to you and to live our lives according to your words and wisdom. Amen.

March 3

Thank you, Lord, for the balm of time that heals our nation's wounds and allows us to press on. Thank you, too, for our national memorials that help us remember our past and what we have experienced together. Let these shared memories of past pain and triumph continue to draw us together and make us strong. Let the hope of our future inspire our imagination and rekindle our vision. But most of all, Father, let the present moment be dedicated to what is most precious and meaningful in life. May America always know how to make each moment count! In your name, amen.

March 4

Holy Father, stand with us as we stand together as one nation, one people, one spirit. Let your presence move through us as we unite in love, peace, and harmony. One nation, one people, one spirit. Express your will in our actions, our words, our thoughts. One nation, one people, one spirit. Direct our steps toward that which spreads love, light, and hope. One nation, one people, one spirit. Stand with us, Lord of Light, as we make our stand for freedom, for liberty, for the pursuit of joy. One nation, one people, one spirit.

★ ★ ★ ★ ★

Hope knows that on the other side of pain is joy and on the other side of injustice is peace.

March 5

Who knows better than you, O Lord, the importance of teach-

ers, for you are the Master Teacher. Our country's teachers are a great national resource. They awaken young minds and give a glimpse of the past so our children may learn to manage the future.

We acknowledge the energy and commitment it takes to work with our children each day, and we pray you will touch each of these women and men with your love and inspire them to greatness.

Keep them in your care, Father. Direct their thoughts and actions toward the benefit of our country. Help us always to encourage our teachers and to give them our greatest respect and our thanks.

March 6

You are eternal, O God!
Your word will endure as long as the heavens shine above us.
We thank you that you have remained faithful to all
    generations and that we can continue to count on you.
Help us to know your teachings, O God.
Your laws are life itself.
Guide us in all we do, and we will try to be
    as faithful to you as you are to us.
Show us your laws, that we may obey you with all our hearts.
We yearn to be your unwavering followers, dear God.
Give us the strength to do what is right and
    to follow closely the path you have prepared for us.
We stand ready to take the path that leads to life.
Show us the way. Amen.

March 7

One of the great strengths of our nation, God, is our ability to produce huge amounts of food. You've blessed us with millions of acres of fertile land from which we draw millions of bushels of life-giving food each year. We praise you for that gift.

We also thank you, God, for the men and women who have worked the ground since the beginning to give us food. It's never been easy, God. The farmers have always depended on you for the right weather and protection from pests to get food out of the ground. And in the years when nothing went right, they've depended on you to get them through to the next year and the next. Thank you for their sacrifice. Thank you for their work ethic and moral courage. Thank you, Father, for American farmers.

March 8

Holy God, we long to feel
your loving breath upon
us, which moves through-
out our innermost being
with your heavenly peace.
When we face trying days,
we often feel worn down
and diminished, but your

comforting presence gives us renewed hope, strength, and
commitment to overcoming any challenges placed in our path.
Spirit, keep us as a good shepherd tends his flock. Help us to
find answers to our questions and solutions to our problems.
Without you we can do little. With you, Holy Spirit, we can do
everything. Amen.

March 9

Thank you, Father, for your great grace toward this nation. Thank you that through your blessings we can in turn bless many other nations with food relief, financial help, military aid, building materials, education, and medical assistance. From large government programs to small summer mission teams, Father, the spectrum of help that goes out around the world is a testimony to the plenty with which you have provided us. Enlarge our concern for those in need, and increase our generosity. For the sake of your graciousness, amen.

★ ★ ★ ★ ☆

This country will not be a good place for any of us to live in unless we make it a good place for all of us to live in.

President Theodore Roosevelt

March 10

Father, thank you for the people
who make up this great big
nation under you. Thank you for
the school children struggling to
learn math, for the grocery store
clerks stocking the shelves, for
the nursing home workers comforting the elderly, for the

accountants working to balance the books, for the runners
trying to master their bodies.

Thank you for the businesspeople who pay their employees a
living wage, for the scientists who keep looking for the next
breakthrough, and for the film directors striving to tell powerful stories with powerful images. Thank you for all the people
working every day to do their part to make America great.

March 11

Awesome God, we admit that sometimes we try to put you in a box so we can understand you. When we realize that other people see you differently than we do, we are forced to take you out of that stifling box to confront you in all your complexity. Your love may be simple, but your power is not.

Help us be open to other people's understanding of you. May we be clear about our own beliefs but open to learn more about you through others' understandings. Even though we are more comfortable with you in the box we have made, we realize that you are beyond our comprehension. Your thoughts are not our thoughts. Your ways are not our ways. You are truly an awesome God, and we kneel before you in gratitude for how you work in our lives. Amen.

March 12

Lord, you have urged each of us to treat our bodies as temples. The people of this nation have heard you and are trying to live healthier lives through exercise and diet.

Our country's emphasis on fitness is a source of pride to all of us. It feels good to be part of a nation that prizes good health.

We owe you our thanks, Heavenly Father, for inspiring us to physical as well as mental well-being.

☆ ☆ ☆ ☆ ☆

Feel the power of living in hope, for it is the place in the heart that lies between dreaming and doing.

March 13

Lord, I ask that you would make the people of our nation as one. I ask that we stand together behind our leaders, behind the ideals upon which we're built, behind our freedom. Give us an appropriate pride in the flag that represents that freedom. Give us warmth of spirit when we come together as Americans in shopping malls and sports stadiums and places of worship. Help us to be bound together for all that is right.

Thank you, God, for the powerful emotions that flood our hearts when we remember what America stands for. I ask that those emotions become actions and words that will make us even stronger in the years to come.

March 14

It's hard for me to believe, dear Lord, that there are still people in other places of the world who must worship you in secret. Their governments do not allow them to sing to you, pray to you, talk about you, express their love for you. Be with the believers in those countries, Lord. Give them comfort and peace and a freedom of spirit that no tyrant can destroy. And as I openly and without fear enter my place of worship this week, help me to pause to thank you for a country in which I can freely choose and practice my faith. Amen.

☆ ☆ ☆ ☆ ☆

When the world around us grows cold and chaotic,
faith is the balm that soothes a fearful heart
and the blanket that comforts an anxious mind.

March 15

Father, when a nation mourns, especially a nation of this size, what do you see from the heavens? Do you see our heavy hearts and weeping souls? Do you see our weary backs and tear-filled eyes? And what do you hear? Do you hear our cries of anguish and gasps of pain? Do you hear our shouts of horror and sighs of helplessness?

Father, we need to know that you see and hear our mourning. Wrap your arms around us; hold us tight. Reassure us that you are aware of our suffering and you are mourning with us. Father, we know that you are not a God of flippant answers. We know that you don't wave a magic wand to make our pain go away. That's okay, God. All that we really want and need right now is the reassurance that you are walking through our mourning with us and that we are not alone. Remind us, Lord, that you are right here beside us. Amen.

March 16

It's a beautiful statue that keeps watch over New York Harbor, Lord God. With her torch held high above her head, she lights the way to this land where freedom still rings. Yes, Lady Liberty continues to herald hope for all who seek refuge from tyranny and oppression. Father, may America always be that place of freedom and reprieve for those who seek it. For the glory of your name, amen.

☆ ☆ ☆ ☆ ☆

For this is what America is all about. It is the uncrossed desert and the unclimbed ridge. It is the star that is not reached and the harvest that is sleeping in the unplowed ground.

President Lyndon B. Johnson, Inaugural Address, January 20, 1965

March 17

Our Father, creator of all things and all people, we sing with joy for the infinite variety you bring to our homeland. We love our diversity, with people of all races and creeds and ethnic backgrounds fusing together as one. Nearly every country on earth can find a piece of itself here.

We are like a gigantic quilt, with patches of different shapes, colors, and patterns stitched together with intricate threads of common experience. Preserve our diversity, Lord, as we bask in the richness of shared customs, foods, literature, and art from around the world.

March 18

Protect our nation from without. From enemies who seek to destroy our homes and land and people—to steal our peace and freedom. From natural disasters of flood, fire, and famine. From disease and hunger and economic upheaval. From accidents in hospitals and on roadways and in the workplace.

But even more, Lord, we ask your protection over our nation from enemies within our borders. Please protect us from our own immorality and hatred and greed. Protect us from compromising our integrity in favor of what's easy. Protect us from our tendency to trust ourselves instead of you.

Lord, I thank you for your protection. I thank you that I can rely on the security of your love, even in times of trouble. Amen.

March 19

God, thank you for the men and women who have willingly served to protect and preserve American freedoms in the past centuries. Thank you for those who fought to give birth to this nation. Thank you for those who fought to preserve the unity of this nation. Thank you for those who gave up comforts, home, family time, luxuries, hobbies, and so much more in their efforts to provide all of us with the freedom to enjoy those very same things. And most important, thank you for those who made the ultimate sacrifice—their own lives—so that freedom and goodness and truth can continue to define the land. Amen.

March 20

Dear God, we are proud of the things that make us uniquely American: the Declaration of Independence, the Constitution, the Statue of Liberty, our patriotic songs. We are proud of how our nation has lent a helping hand to other nations throughout the world and of our willingness to share our bounty. We are proud of our image as a melting pot. This pride is natural in so great a nation, yet we realize that Americans need more than pride. Help us know when to be humble.

Forgive us those times when our arrogance has built walls when we should have been constructing bridges. Open us to other peoples and other nations so we can all work for peace without measuring which nation gives the most. Let us continue to be proud of our nation even as we acknowledge actions that may have been hurtful to others. Guide us to live with all people on earth in harmony. Amen.

March 21

Father, I glory in the precious gift of freedom you've lavished on our nation. Freedom to worship you. Freedom to speak our minds. Freedom to meet together to worship. Many around the world don't understand it because they've never tasted it.

Help us never take that freedom for granted, God. Help us appreciate the freedom that we have in you and the freedom of being Americans. And help us use our freedom for the good of all, never for wrong. Thank you, God, for our freedom.

☆ ☆ ☆ ☆ ☆

Sometimes people call me an idealist. Well, that is the way I know I am an American. . . . America is the only idealistic nation in the world.

President Woodrow Wilson

March 22

God, lately I've found myself feeling discouraged about the subtle messages that shape the values of many Americans. They say: If only you had more money, you'd be happier. If only you had more things, you'd be content. If only you bought this or that, you'd be satisfied. If only you climbed the ladder of success, you'd be gratified. If only you would spend more time thinking about yourself, you'd be more cheerful.

There is only one way to combat this philosophy—take time each day to say, "Thanks, God, for a house that keeps me dry in the rain, for a school that teaches my children, for a coat that keeps out the chill, for shoes that protect my toes, and for a grocery store that sells good food." So, God, I'm saying thanks for those things and a million other little things that make life livable, bearable, enjoyable, and magnificent. Amen.

March 23

You have commanded us, God, not to set our hopes on riches but on you. Daily, you provide us with all we need. In return,

you appeal to us to be generous in good works and ready to share.

Americans have long been known for their generosity and willingness to share. We swell with emotion when we see strangers helping strangers in time of need, gathering goods and food and money. They inspire us to do the same.

We thank you, Father, that we live in a country where citizens freely open their hearts and their pockets in your name.

March 24

Dear God, I know America isn't a single thing. We're a nation of states. And our states comprise regions. And those regions contain cities and towns and villages. And those towns comprise neighborhoods. And in the neighborhoods, blocks. And on those blocks, houses filled with families.

Father, I ask that you make America strong by strengthening its families. And through those families, its neighborhoods, its cities, and its states. And through those, the strength of these United States. I ask that our nation grow stronger and stronger.

Lord, I ask your help to begin by teaching me to love my family and to be a good neighbor.

March 25

Thank you, Father, for clothing, shelter, and food. Thank you for a warm shower, a cold drink, a soft bed. This country affords so much physical comfort and convenience, and I don't always remember to be grateful. I drive on good roads, use public libraries, and get my mail delivered. Thank you that the taxes I pay come back to me in life-enhancing ways. I know things aren't perfect in the United States, but I still believe that, all in all, it's the best place in the world to live. So as I think on all my blessings, Lord, fill my heart with a consistent gratitude for all that I have here. Amen.

☆ ☆ ☆ ☆ ☆

In moments of awe and wonder, we become re-enchanted with the magic of our everyday lives—magic that is ever-present but often overlooked.

March 26

Lord, today the scent of spring is in the air, fresh and breezy, light and free in all its green expectancy.

Soon gardens will burst into bloom: daffodils pushing through the damp earth . . . enough to make a Wordsworth dream come true. A host of golden-hooded glories to greet the sun! The woodlands will fill with deep gentian bluebells, then the first willow buds and tiny hedge roses. Lord, I can hardly wait!

So much promise, Lord. So much growth. There is so much hope in our hearts in springtime.

Help us, also, to bring forth our promise and bloom, to show ourselves in all our glory. Give us the strength to grow and flourish. Let us bring joy and promise to our world, as you do. Lord, I can hardly wait!

March 27

Under the night sky, Lord, I feel very small and insignificant. Of the millions and millions of people in this country, I am a mere speck of humanity. I sometimes feel that I've only been counted, not named. I have a phone number, a PIN number, a credit card number, a social security number, a driver's license number, a medical insurance number, an employee number, a frequent flyer number, a checking account number, a library patron number, a voice mail retrieval number. There are model and serial numbers on my microwave, my washer and dryer, my television, my bicycle, my car, my computer, my screen door. I live in a world of numbers, infinite and cold.

Thank goodness, Lord, that you know my name and that in this sea of people, I am more than simply "present and counted." I am loved and named.

March 28

God, what makes a nation strong? Is it money? Is it armies? Is it pride? No, Lord. Our nation's strength is its people who have worked hard and suffered so our country could grow.

We honor the people from the present and the past, who, with you at their sides, have made our land great. May we follow in their footsteps, Lord, and be worthy of the name "American".

☆　☆　☆　☆　☆

America! America!
God shed his grace on thee
And crown thy good with brotherhood
From sea to shining sea!

Katherine Lee Bates, "America the Beautiful"

March 29

Bring your justice to the world, O Lord.
Do not let evildoers go free, laughing at those they have hurt.
Bring your justice to the world, O Lord.
Help us know it is not our job to have revenge in our hearts.
Bring your justice to the world, O Lord.
Help us know when we have hurt others.
Bring your justice to the world, O Lord.
Don't let us even unknowingly side with those who do evil.
Bring your justice to the world, O Lord.
Guide us in all we do, that we may always work
    for what is right.
We long for your justice, O Lord.

March 30

God, we have become so accustomed to our freedoms, we have been lulled into apathy. We've nearly forgotten what it took to obtain those freedoms and to keep our country independent. Wars, loss of life, and deprivation have visited us all too often. When we are awakened to the possibilities of losing our way of

 life, our freedoms become instantly dearer.

Forgive us, Father, for taking our democracy and our good life for granted.

Bless and protect our native land. Help us, we pray, to regain our patriotic fervor and to preserve our country for the generations to come.

March 31

God, in our efforts to improve life through technological advances, we run the risk of making life more complicated than it once was. Our phones, computers, pagers, and handhelds perform infinite tasks, but at the same time, we run the risk of being enslaved by their abilities. Those things that are meant to make life easier for us sometimes make life muddy and stressful and out of control.

Help us to find the balance between our ever-advancing lifestyle and simplicity. Don't let us become controlled by a piece of equipment that has no identity, no soul, and no personality. Help our lives remain simple even as we strive to become wiser. Amen.

April 1

The time of hope and renewal dawns in America: in our gardens, in the trees, and in the celebration of resurrection. Restore our joy, Father, where we have been robbed of it. Bring healing to our hearts where we have been wounded by evil. Grant us a fresh surge of strength to rebuild where we have been torn down. And let us rise up in your power, as a testimony to your promise of new life to all who trust in you.

★ ★ ★ ☆ ☆

We shall steer safely through every storm, so long as our heart is right, our intention fervent, our courage steadfast, and our trust fixed on God.

St. Francis of Sales

April 2

Lord, watch over the children tonight. Let them sleep safe and warm and unaware of the turmoil and confusion in the world today. Shelter and protect them, that they may grow to know a better world someday. Let not their tiny hearts know fear, anxiety, worry, or grief but only hope and love. Amen.

☆　☆　☆　☆　☆

Faith is a true sign of bravery. It is looking forward to the future despite challenges and adversity. It is trusting in something that you can neither see nor touch, yet you know it is always there to guide you along life's path.

April 3

O Holy One, we pray for the souls of innocent people who have died in acts of violence. In memory of those who were killed by guns in the street, we pray for peace. In memory of those whose lives were ended by acts of terrorism, we pray for peace. In memory of every woman, man, or child who died because of the hatred in another's heart, we pray for peace.

Keep these valiant souls foremost in our hearts and minds that we might honor their memory, and because of how they died, we pledge ourselves to live in peace. Wash our hearts that they may be whiter than snow, and put all thoughts of violence far from our minds. Give us the strength to say: "Peace starts here, with me, in my heart." Inspire us to act so that others might put aside their own violent thoughts. Guide us toward concrete actions that lead to peace, so that someday we might live as one people in peace. In your holy name we pray, amen.

April 4

Lord, you often speak to us through dreams. Through our dreams, you fill us with your Spirit. You whisper your will and wisdom and call us to act for the good of others in your glorious name.

Dreams of faith and freedom carried the first Americans across a wide and raging ocean. Dreams of hope and liberty led our ancestors to this beautiful country and helped them make it our home. Dreams of justice gave our people strength and conviction to fight for the weak wherever they might be in the world.

We are proud to be citizens of a country founded on dreams.

April 5

Heavenly Father, with happy hearts we praise you for the beauty of our country in springtime: for the awakening of life, for the refreshment of rain, for the promise of good things to come.

We have lived through a time of darkness, but winter is past. Life is beginning anew. You come to us like the rains that water the earth or the soft breezes that caress our cheeks.

It is a time of singing throughout our land, and you stir up in us songs of hope, songs of love, and songs of joy.

April 6

God, I look at before-and-after photos of our presidents, and I realize how stressful their time in office must have been. You can see it in the changed expressions on their faces and in the looks in their eyes. I imagine the sleepless nights and long meetings agonizing over matters of life and death. I imagine hours of self-doubt, second-guessing, and weighing the words of critics. I imagine all the distractions of politics.

Please, God, give our president wisdom and courage to do what's right for our nation. Help him choose the best course of action over the popular. Help his advisors to be faithful, honest, and insightful. Protect him from our enemies, and guide him to your hope. Thank you for this president. Help him sleep well tonight.

April 7

Father, thank you for the rich diversity with which you have blessed this nation—for the cities and the farms, for the mountains and the valleys, for the heat and the cold, for the oceans and the deserts, for the forests and the plains, for the sand and the snow, for the new and the old, for the day and the

night, for the sun and the moon, for the stars and the clouds.

Most of all, thank you for the rich diversity of our people—for the colors, the sizes, the ages, the talents, the names, and the heritage. Help us appreciate this diversity for what it really is—an amazing gift and opportunity to know and love a multitude of your precious creations. Amen.

April 8

Lord, as our country's leaders deal with national problems, we commit them to your care and ask you to be with them. Keep them strong, and help them make the right decisions. Let common sense prevail. Guide them in the ways of peace.

Bless us, the citizens of the United States, with patience and understanding, and enable us to respond in a spirit of cooperation to the decisions made by our representatives. Amen.

★ ★ ★ ★ ☆

What we need are critical lovers of America—patriots who express their faith in their country by working to improve it.

Hubert H. Humphrey,
Beyond Civil Rights: A New Day of Equality

April 9

I thank you, Lord, for amber waves of grain. For grocery shelves filled with cereal and macaroni and cheese. This is a land of plenty, a land of farms both large and small that feed our country as well as many parts of the world. So we thank you for our daily bread. Be with our farmers, and give them strength and joy. We are blessed, and we are grateful. Amen.

★ ★ ★ ★ ☆

A nation that works together thrives together.

April 10

Lady Liberty stands at the gates of America welcoming all who seek refuge on her blessed shores. Her torch is the freedom people long for, her crown the liberty they seek to live their lives under. She guides the huddled, weary masses to the land of opportunity, the land of dreams come true. We are thankful for her, for being the symbol of an entire nation and for giving hope to those who were hopeless and a home to those who were homeless. God, we thank you for this great symbol of our land.

★　★　★　★　☆

Democracy is a seed borne on the winds of freedom.

April 11

Dear Father, honest peo-
ple often disagree about
the direction our country
should go. They stake out
positions that are directly
opposed to each other,
each believing theirs is the

better way for our great nation to grow stronger. Fierce words
are exchanged; our leaders are divided.

Father, I ask that you give wisdom to those who lead and to
all who vote for our leaders. I pray that you allow us to disagree
in peace and to move together toward choices that honor you.
I ask that you help our leaders to know when to compromise
and when to refuse to budge. Please, Father, bring our nation
together.

April 12

Lord, it only takes a moment to close our eyes and imagine how our country must look from your point of view: the wide blue skies, the wind rippling the prairie grasses, the mountains tall against the horizon, and the glistening lakes.

America truly is beautiful!

And in our city streets, amid the bustle and haste, there is loveliness, too. You inspire us to create churches, libraries, parks, schools, museums, and homes to fulfill our daily needs.

Yes, America truly is beautiful!

Lord, remind us we can find beauty wherever we look. Remind us that wherever we walk, we walk on your earth. All the earth is holy ground and beautiful!

April 13

I pray today for comfort, Lord. I pray for knowledge to help make informed decisions. I pray for guidance to lead us to a better country. I pray today for love to make the world a better place.

☆ ☆ ☆ ☆ ☆

As we have recaptured and rekindled our pioneering spirit, we have insisted that it shall always be a spirit of justice, a spirit of teamwork, a spirit of sacrifice, and above all, a spirit of neighborliness.

President Franklin D. Roosevelt, October 4, 1933

April 14

Lord, give me a heart full of courage and steadfast faith. Make me a soldier in your army of compassion and a warrior of caring and concern. Let me be a light in the darkness, a beacon of hope to inspire others. Make me an instrument of your peace and a channel for your infinite love. Amen.

☆ ☆ ☆ ☆ ☆

Not one of us can be free unless our fellow citizens are also free.

April 15

Heavenly Father, you say, "I have called you by name; you are mine." It encourages and comforts me to know of your specific and all-encompassing love. You extend to all humankind the same measure of abundant love. Help me remember that every human being is my brother or my sister, that in our human family we have a responsibility to one another.

Thank you for the generosity of America and the programs our government has to help the less fortunate, both in our country and in poorer lands. Help me have a glad heart at tax time when I realize how much of my income goes to helping people who have so little. Remind me each time I think I could use that money myself that you say, "To whom much is given, much is expected." Amen.

U.S. Capitol building

April 16

Creator and Author of Life, we see signs of your newness
    all around us.

Help us as Americans to claim the newness that is
    possible in you.

You are our refreshment and hope.

You are the creative spirit that dwells in each of us.

You are the spark for each idea that comes to us
    and the energy for enacting our ideas.

May we as citizens and leaders of these United States look
always for innovative solutions to old problems. May we find
new perspectives and positive attitudes when it comes to personal relationships or international conflicts.

You give life. Everything is new in you.

Let us also be new, creative, transformed. Amen.

April 17

The world is bursting with life today. The crocus is peeking out from beneath your soil, the chirps of tiny birds are heard for the first time as life is witnessed everywhere from ground to tree limbs to sky. Help me, dear God, to live my day like that of a newborn—without judgment and with acceptance. Spring is a time to begin again. Guide me to a new way of living. Help me see our beautiful world through the eyes of a child—freely and willingly. Amen.

★ ★ ★ ★ ☆

Hope gives wings to the wishes of the soul.

April 18

God, I took some time today to do nothing. Actually, I did a thousand things—I read, I thought, I daydreamed, I breathed deeply, I strolled, I hummed, I lifted my face to the sun so I could drink in its warmth. But most of these things are considered nonessentials in this fast-paced world of ours. Help me do nothing more often. Help me sit still and listen to the world around me. Help me focus on you so that I stay

grounded in truth. Help me just *be* often enough so that I am able to *do* the things that I'm responsible for. And help me encourage others to both *be* and *do* as well. Amen.

April 19

Heavenly Father, our country has enjoyed the highest level of freedom of any country in the world. For that we thank and praise you.

We have the Constitution and the Bill of Rights to guarantee our freedom to speak without fear, worship you, choose our leaders, oppose wrongs, and defend what is right. Americans enjoy these freedoms because you have been with us, Lord, guiding our leaders and ordinary citizens to do extraordinary things in your name.

Continue to give us your guidance and your strength to resist those forces that would take away our precious freedoms and pull us down to their level. Humbly we ask you to preserve our country's freedoms so that we may remain a beacon of light to the world.

April 20

Spirit, the children need you. Give them a peaceful slumber, full of dreams of hope and wonder and childish pleasures. If they should awaken in the middle of the night and cry out in fear, comfort them with your loving presence, that they may know they are protected and cared for throughout the long, dark hours. And when they rise to face a new day, shine your light upon them, that they may feel the joy of being young, free, and blessed. Thank you, Spirit.

☆ ☆ ☆ ☆ ☆

Our gift to our children is the faith of our founders.

April 21

If only people looked at each other with respect instead of
    jealousy...
If only people saw each other as friends instead of enemies...
If only it wasn't one nation under God but one world
    under God...
Then this would be heaven on earth.

Please, Lord, forgive us our mistakes and judgmental thoughts,
and guide us to be the best people and nation we can be.
Amen.

☆   ☆   ☆   ☆   ☆

*Though Americans with differing viewpoints sometimes are
opponents, we must never think of each other as enemies.
We are all Americans.*

April 22

You, O God, gave us this great country with all the rich natural resources we treasure: forests, waters, wind, coal, mountains, oil. Help us to treasure also the greatest resource of the United States: her people.

Thank you for those whose faces are the color of peaches, café au lait, or rich honey; those with blue eyes or brown; those who speak Tagalag or Korean or Spanish as well as English. Thank you for scientists, educators, garbage collectors, nurses, environmentalists, hairdressers, and public servants. Thank you for people whose ancestors have been here for generations and for those who have only recently sojourned to this land of freedom. Let us all join together in gratitude for each other and for the gifts we each bring to our nation. In your great name we pray, amen.

April 23

God, I praise you for the great spirit of exploration you've instilled in the hearts of Americans. From the courageous pilgrims who endured an ocean to land on barren shores in search of freedom, to the pioneers who pushed into and through the wilderness of the West to find opportunity, to the astronauts who strap themselves to rockets to be propelled to the moon and beyond.

What wonderful things you've allowed us to find, Lord. We can only imagine the new discoveries that await as we push up into space, down into oceans, and deeper into our own cells. Thank you, Lord, for the great missions you've granted us. Help us to fulfill them with your blessing; let us honor you, dear God, with what we find.

April 24

Lord, we Americans are compassionate, peace-loving people. When we see need, we rally and act to fulfill that need. When we see injustice, we stand together and speak out to call for change. We know, Lord, that peace and compassion call for action and not just words.

Today, we ask you to let your love and compassion flow into our lives and out into the world through us and our actions. Make us instruments of your peace, in the truest sense of the word.

☆ ☆ ☆ ☆ ☆

A hero is an ordinary person who works against extraordinary odds to make the impossible a reality.

April 25

Father, I'm amazed when I think of the pioneers breaking new ground on the American prairie. What courageous men and women they must have been. They moved into the land and occupied it. They set up borders. They coaxed life from new soil. They planted crops. They grew cities out of empty acres. They sacrificed their lives to build this nation, God.

Thank you for guiding their work, for protecting them, for comforting them in their losses, for seeing them through to eventual success. Thank  you, Father, for the spirit that allowed them to establish a great nation from the Atlantic all the way across the plains and the mountains to the Pacific.

April 26

What will your children have tomorrow, God? It's so easy to get caught up in the here and now that we often forget to think about tomorrow. Will the sun shine as brightly for our grandchildren? Will the summer breezes feel as warm? There have been great changes since the birth of our country and our world. May we continue to move forward with positive steps—one step at a time. Amen.

★ ★ ★ ★ ☆

America is only as strong as her families.
If we lose the ability to hold those families together,
we risk losing America as we know it.

April 27

God, at this very moment, thank you
    for the teachers who are teaching our children,
    for the doctors who are treating our sick,
    for the farmers who are sowing our food,
    for the judges who are protecting our laws,
    for the police who are watching our streets,
    for the firefighters who are saving our lives,
    for the carpenters who are building our homes,
    for the postal employees who are sorting our mail,
    for the cobblers who are resoling our shoes,
    for the students who are studying our past,
    for the janitors who are cleaning our schools,
    for the gardeners who are maintaining our parks,
    for the engineers who are designing our roads,
    and for all the other people who make life not only
        possible but precious. Amen.

April 28

God, our armed forces have been trained to protect our country in war and peace. They place their trust in you. We pray now that you would protect them as they fulfill their promises.

These gallant citizens make untold sacrifices to keep our homes and country safe. They pledged to give their lives, if necessary, to defend the principles that made our country free.

Honor their commitment and their courage, Father, as you encourage us to do the same.

Each one of them is precious to us, as they are to you. Comfort them and the families from whom they are separated. Give them strength, guidance, and conviction as they face the unknown with the name of God and country on their lips and in their hearts.

April 29

Thank you, Lord, for music. For country music and rock music and rap music. Thank you for Handel and Bach, for Elvis and The Beatles. Thank you for marching bands and jazz bands and everything in between.

"Make a joyful noise to the Lord, all the earth; break forth into joyous song and sing praises," the Scriptures say (Psalm 98:4), and I am glad to do it. Thank you for stores filled with CDs and radio stations filled with songs. Thank you for old hymns and new praise songs. Give me a song today. In this and every way I give you praise. Amen.

★ ★ ★ ★ ☆

To be an American is to be free to dance to a tune only you can hear, to march to a drumbeat all your own.

April 30

God, thank you for giving our leaders, past and present, the eyes to see that you created people to be free. Thank you for helping them realize that nothing should take away that freedom—not skin color, not race, not ethnic background.

 "We hold these truths to be self-evident," they wrote, "that all men are created equal."

Father, I thank you for creating us free and equal. I ask that you would continue to heal past wounds of racial inequality and prevent new wounds of racial strife. Please give us a unity as Americans that is bolstered by the diversity of our ethnicity. Please make it self-evident to *all* of us that you made us to become one nation under you.

May 1

The cherry blossoms in our nation's capital are turning their faces toward the gentle touch of your spring sunshine, Blessed Creator. How beautiful are your works! They adorn our national monuments like garlands of peace and blessing. How we long for your continued kindness to us, Lord. Cause your goodness to blossom in the heart of our nation. Begin with me, Lord, as I turn my face toward the gentle touch of your transforming grace. Amen.

☆ ☆ ☆ ☆ ☆

The names of the states themselves form a chorus of sweet and most romantic vocables: Delaware, Ohio, Indiana, Florida, Dakota, Iowa, Wyoming, Minnesota, and the Carolinas.

Robert Louis Stevenson, *Across the Plains*

May 2

God, as I go about this day, open my heart to blessings I seldom notice—the shadow of a leaf dancing on a wall, sunlight sparkling in a puddle, the giggle of a child, the bold stripes of our nation's flag. Thank you, God, for all that reminds me of the joys of being your child and being free. Amen.

☆ ☆ ☆ ☆ ☆

You're a grand old flag, you're a high flying flag.
And forever in peace may you wave.
You're the emblem of the land I love,
The home of the free and the brave.
Ev'ry heart beats true under red, white, and blue,
Where there's never a boast or brag.

George M. Cohan, "You're a Grand Old Flag"

May 3

Lord, in times of trouble, the pain can be so deep that words are no comfort. What can we say to someone who has lost a loved one? What will help?

Perhaps silence is the correct response. If words can't help and heal, Lord, enfold and protect us with your cloak of peace. Help us share stillness with one another. Guide us to the place where we can simply *be* without doing—present and prayerful, comforted and quiet in your presence until we heal.

★ ★ ★ ★ ☆

When bad things happen in our country, we become aware of the fragility of life and the importance of loving and caring for one another. We grieve for those who are suffering, as if millions of hearts are beating as one.

May 4

God,
be my strength and shield.
Show me your love every day.
Guide me from the moment I wake
    until I fall into sleep at the end of the day.
Bless me that I might do your work on earth.
Let me live so that when my time is complete
    I might joyfully return to you.
You are my God, and I love you now and always. Amen.

May 5

God, some have called America a great experiment. Can a nation of free people govern themselves? Can they remain free and powerful and organized around one set of ideals? So far, God, so good. You've blessed us well beyond what we could ever have done for ourselves. You've made America the greatest nation on earth.

God, I ask that you keep reminding us that we need you and that you are the source of our success as a nation. Please help us to always remember what you've done for us and what you would have us do for you. Please help us be a nation that points the world to you, God, and not just to ourselves.

May 6

Lord, let us not forget what it means to be an American. Let us not silence those who speak against us—let us promote free speech. Let us not censor the art of those we do not understand—let us promote free expression. Let us not show prejudice against those who worship a different God—let us promote freedom of religion. Let us promote the freedom of every citizen to pursue justice, liberty, and happiness.

★ ★ ★ ★ ☆

It is in trying times that a nation's true colors shine through.

May 7

Thank you, Father, for this free and diverse people. Bless this melting pot, and season it with your grace.

Bridge the gaps between us, and heal our broken hearts. Take away our suspicion, and help us see each other as you see us— not white or black or brown or yellow, Christian or Jew or Muslim, male or female—as people who need each other and need you.

Help us celebrate our differences. Amen.

☆ ☆ ☆ ☆ ☆

Many homelands but only one home.
Many ethnic backgrounds but only one citizenship.
Many philosophies but one freedom that protects us all.

May 8

Lord, thank you for all the mothers in America. Thank you for those who are at the workplace, faithfully providing for their families. As they balance deadlines, coworkers, supervisors, and all the duties that fill their days, give them a sense of peace about their children's care and well being. Bless the people who are watching the children of the mothers at work.

Thank you for the mothers who are at home, faithfully providing for their families. As they balance schedules, sibling interactions, and all the duties that fill their days, give them a sense of peace about their own care and well-being. And help all mothers, wherever they may be, to appreciate each other's sacrifices and to respect their different decisions. Certainly, all mothers are deserving of our greatest thanks and admiration. Amen.

May 9

I drove home yesterday evening and viewed the most awesome sight: the red, white, and blue banner of America waving against the black night sky, with a full gray moon off to the side. The flag seemed to be waving its freedom defiantly. I realized then that we will remain the home of the free through the dark of night and the light of day until you, O mighty God, decide otherwise.

☆ ☆ ☆ ☆ ☆

"The land of the free and the home of the brave" is more than a description of America—it is a definition of life as it should be lived by all humanity.

May 10

Listening God, out of the fullness of our hearts we pray to you.
You alone are holy. You alone are wise.
It seems that just when we think we have it all figured out,
    something happens that disrupts our calm and calls
      everything we know into question.
And we turn to you. We are not alone.
You know our needs before we express them;
    your love reaches out to us even when we ignore you.
Bless us. Comfort us.
Keep us connected to you and your holy wisdom.
Help us never to forget that your love can sustain us when the
world crashes down around our feet and to realize we don't
know it all, can't do it all, can survive only with your strength.
Listening God, out of the fullness of our hearts we pray to you.
Amen.

May 11

God, America is more than just millions of people. We're also millions of families. Some of those families have been here since the first boats arrived. Others are disembarking today,

ready to start brand new lives on our shores. But, Lord, you know our nation will never be stronger than our families.

So, God, I ask that you make the families of this nation strong. Help moms and dads build on the foundation of your truth. Help them grow in your love. Help them remain committed to each other. Help younger family members honor and respect those who are older. Help older members impart honest wisdom to the young. Help all families be bound in warm unity and deep love.

May 12

We are what we are, Lord, and we are Americans. You decree all things, and you decreed that we should be citizens of this noble country.

We're proud of our country and who we are. Proud of the freedom to do as we please, as long as we do no evil. We appreciate the good things in life and pray only that you save us from the temptations of greed. We're grateful for the right to speak out and say what we think, as long as we speak the truth. We're thankful we may praise your name openly and without fear. Though we bow our heads when we come before you, let us hold our heads high in the eyes of the world. For we are your people, custodians of a land created by your hands.

We are what we are, Lord. We're Americans, and what we ask, we ask from our hearts: God Bless America.

May 13

Lord, we pray for all people in want throughout our land. Despite the richness of our country, there are many who are needy in our communities. You have commanded us to care for those less fortunate.

Give us compassion as we deal with the problems of poverty, hunger, and homelessness. Let "the land of the free" include everyone within our borders.

In times of national emergency, these domestic problems become even more intense. Lend us your insights, Father, as we attempt to solve this dilemma. Give us wisdom to find solutions, and impress upon us the urgency of this mission.

Above all, teach us to give more of ourselves in your name.

May 14

Dear God, today I am thinking of paths. How easy it is to take the path already smoothed by other feet, where all the rocks have been removed, all the holes filled in, and signs already mark the way. But maybe that is not the path you would have me take today. Help me to make a path where I ought to be rather than the one already paved. Our country's pioneers did this. Thank you for their vision and their courage, their commitment that, in the end, populated our country from sea to sea.

Although my path may be but a dim reflection of those pioneers' trails, I ask for the vision and courage to risk exploring a wilderness instead of following the ways of others. Amen.

☆ ☆ ☆ ☆ ☆

Our votes are cast into our nation's future, not into a vacuum.

May 15

Father, we read American history in books and watch it on TV. But millions of people in America hold that history in their heads and hearts. They've lived the last sixty, seventy, eighty or more years of our national story. Thank you, Lord, for these

touchstones to our past who have learned wisdom from the best teacher— experience.

Help the rest of us, Lord, honor and respect those older than ourselves. Give us the time and patience to stop and listen to what they have to say. Help us shower them with both national and personal honor. And help America grow stronger as we practice the wisdom of our elders.

May 16

When we don't know what else to say, the best thing is often a simple, heartfelt "thank you." So, Lord . . .

Thank you for your Living Word. It brings us comfort and teaches us to live with integrity.

Thank you for your promise of eternal life. It soothes our souls and makes us strive to be worthy.

Thank you for your divine wisdom. It guides our paths and teaches us to reach for the highest truth.

Thank you for your gift of prayer. It helps us feel less lonely and teaches us to reflect on our thoughts and actions.

You have poured out rich blessings on our lives. Thank you.

May 17

In you we trust, dear God. In you we put our faith, our hope, our dreams for a better tomorrow. Thy will be done, for thy will is always the highest and the best. We stand before you, humbled and willing to do whatever you put in our hearts to do. Direct our paths that we may walk assuredly and confidently along the way set out before us. And let our footprints mark the way for those who come after us, generations to follow who share our dream for a strong and caring nation. In you we trust, dear God. In you we place our lives. Thy will be done. Amen.

☆ ☆ ☆ ☆ ☆

Hope is about believing with a humble heart that tomorrow can be different. It's about knowing that light will come to chase away the darkness.

May 18

Thank you for good roads, stretched out along the coast; for mountains; and for wide and fertile plains. So many people have only rutted trails. We have ribbons of roads to take us to work and play. Thank you for interstates and country lanes. Thank you for police officers and crossing guards. Thank you for traffic lights and stop signs. Thank you for safe roads.

Keep me safe today, Lord God, and guard my family and my friends. Lead us safely home. We give you praise. Amen.

☆ ☆ ☆ ☆ ☆

To be an American is to dream the impossible dream
and then make it happen.
To be an American is to imagine the unimaginable
and then make it real.

May 19

I am in total awe of my country. It is a nation like no other. It prides itself on freedoms and holds itself together with loving acceptance of all its differences. God, please help me to honor and protect my home. God bless America. Amen.

★ ★ ★ ★ ★

We go forth all to seek America. And in the seeking we create her. In the quality of our search shall be the nature of the America that we created.

Waldo Frank, *Our America*

May 20

We map the passage of our lives by our rituals, great and small. Our rituals can be simple and personal or elaborate and valid for an entire nation. Our life maps are shaped by the celebration of births, baptisms, graduations, marriages, and rites of passing. The passing of our years is measured in feasts and holy days.

We need our rituals. They give us comfort, community, and a feeling of belonging. Our feasts also give us purpose, direction, and the knowledge we have something to share with each other.

Prayer is like that. A daily prayer time helps us feel closer to you, Lord, and makes us feel part of the family of God. Encourage us to create and keep our daily rituals of prayer so that we always know when and where we are on the map of our lives.

May 21

We pray for those who live in cities, O God, who live surrounded by tall buildings and bustling crowds. We pray for people who live in rural areas as well—for those who appreciate verdant fields of crops and earthy fragrances.

We pray for those who live in luxury and those who struggle in poverty, for the people who are gainfully employed and those who beg for change. We pray for the ones without friends and for those who confidently assume everyone loves them.

We are all Americans. We are all connected. Help us feel that bond. If we have plenty, inspire us to share. If we are happy and content, remind us to reach out to others. If we are literate, may we work that all might read. We do not live for ourselves alone; help us to work for "liberty and justice for all." Amen.

May 22

Dear God, the world beyond our shores offers so many wonderful sights, so much rich history. But those who travel abroad and then return to the United States describe great emotion at setting foot on American soil again. The whole

world is your creation, Father, but this nation is the one we call home.

Thank you for this home among the nations. Thank you for all our brothers and sisters who live here with us. Thank you for blessing our home, for protecting it, and for making us strong. Thank you for blessing me with such a beautiful home while I wait to join you in my true home forever.

May 23

Help us to be the best we can be, Lord. We sometimes forget how special we are among nations and how we can use our power for good in the world. We sometimes forget that economic interests are not as important as human interests and that our monetary might can save lives if we are willing to share it with those in need.

Help us remember that although we are free, others live in fear and oppression. Let us be symbols of hope to those who long to live as we do. We are lamps of light to people in dark places. We are ambassadors of dreams to those who dare not express themselves. We are warriors of the spirit of love, peace, and the pursuit of happiness to those who know only basic human survival. Don't let us forget, Lord, who we are and what we have to offer.

May 24

Lord, we're a nation of collectors. We all keep mementos of people and events in our lives: a photograph, an item of jewelry, a stone from a secret place. Sometimes the things that bring back memories are less tangible. The smells of a scent that someone wore, baby powder, and home-baked apple pie can carry us back to the places and people we love.

We can't know what others will remember of us when we're gone. We can't know which of all the things we shared will become their memories and mementos. What we can do is live our lives so others will be able to look back on us with love.

Lord, help us always to live our lives so we'll be well remembered. Show us how to be loving, just, and faithful to friends, to family, and to you. Today, let us create lives that will become happy memories for us and those we love.

May 25

O God, our great teacher, few countries on earth have educational opportunities like our own. How blessed we are that every child has the right to an  education and public schools are available to all.

As you helped our country develop, you instilled in your people the importance of learning. You have provided parents as the first teachers and schools to continue the job.

You have inspired our leaders to build libraries and cultural institutions. Help us always to keep the light of learning burning brightly in our land.

May 26

Heavenly Father, Lord above, God of all things seen and unseen, my heart is full of praise that you have given me a life of freedom and abundance, a life built upon the sacrifices of our founders. It would be easy to be smug and say, "Thank you for not putting me in harm's way by making me a citizen of a failing nation torn by war and plagued by hunger." But smugness never fed a hungry child or waved a flag of peace. Lord, as a citizen of this great land, I have a responsibility to share my blessings. In some small way and through your grace, show me how to share today. Amen.

★ ★ ★ ★ ☆

He loves his country best who strives to make it best.

Robert G. Ingersoll, in a speech given on May 29, 1882

May 27

I wake up today, God, and I stare out the window at the beautiful day you've given me. The sun gives an orange hue to all it touches. Birds can be heard in the trees above, while the leaves and blossoms of plants sway gently in the breeze. It is truly a blessing to experience your wondrous works every day. Thank you, God, for this day. Amen.

☆ ☆ ☆ ☆ ☆

Hope blooms like a beautiful rose amidst the thorns of life.

May 28

O Lord, as we celebrate Memorial Day, let me remember that if it was not for the brave people of yesterday, I would not stand free today. Life would not be a gift but, instead, a prison. Not everyone knows the freedoms of life, liberty, and happiness as I do. Today, I thank you, O mighty God, and I thank the heroes of America's past. Help me to have the courage and bravery of my fellow Americans—past and present.

☆ ☆ ☆ ☆ ☆

And so, my fellow Americans: ask not what your country can do for you—ask what you can do for your country.

President John F. Kennedy, Inaugural Address

May 29

Thank you, Lord, for pilgrims, pioneers, and astronauts—for all those who take risks so that we can follow. There is a spirit of adventure in our land, a thirst for the noble and the new.

Thank you for the blessings we enjoy because someone else had the courage to go first. And help us be more like them. Give me an adventure today, God. Give me some new place to go or some small new thing to do. Then give me the courage I need to follow in the footsteps of those who made us free. Amen.

May 30

Loving God, in whom we all are family, please give a special protection to those sisters and brothers who serve in the Armed Forces. Bless them in all they do, and give them courage to face the difficult task of protecting our nation and democracy around the world.

Even though they are called to function as part of a unified body, give them each as individuals compassion, integrity, and a clear sense of purpose. When they are far from home, help them feel love and support from across the distance. Protect them when they are in physical danger. Surround those in the Armed Services with your love and power. As for those of us who live free under their protection, help us remember to offer our gratitude for the important job that these men and women do on behalf of the United States of America. Amen.

May 31

Lord, we thrive on hope. We all dream of love, fulfillment, appreciation, and simple happiness. With your help, there's a lot we can do to make our dreams come true.

We must prepare the ground in our hearts. Then we have to plant our seeds and nurture them as they grow. When the first shoots push through, we must free the patch from the weeds of unfair demands and ridiculous expectations that choke our growth. Then, when our hopes come to fruition, they will be vibrant and strong. We will reap our harvest and share fruits with others, to encourage and inspire them, too.

Lord, help us look within and find our true hopes: the things to which we feel called and the creative acts we need to do to be abundant people. Help us sow and tend the seeds of hope.

June 1

Summer is coming, bringing with it some classic American pleasures, such as baseball, picnics, lemonade stands, hot dogs, apple pie, ice-cream cones, bicycling, outdoor concerts, family reunions, and two-week vacations.

Thank you, Lord, for these and so many traditions that capture the lighthearted, joyful essence of our nation's spirit. Remind me to stop and buy some lemonade from the neighborhood kids. Slow me down enough to attend a baseball game with a friend or neighbor and to enjoy the company of the other fans around me. Help me to appreciate the change in scenery and the new people I meet on my vacation. Let me rejoice in America and Americans this summer.

June 2

Great Spirit, the native people of this place we call America
have taught us to respect the land as though it were alive.
Teach us your ways, God, that we may become one with all of

life around us, that we
may protect our precious
resources and the natural
beauty of our environ-
ment. Show us how to
give back to the land, as
the land has so graciously

and generously given to us. Instill in us a reverence for the air,
the water, the animals, and the green trees that you have given
us dominion over. We thank you, Spirit, for the living earth we
walk upon, for the breathing sky we gaze upon, for America.

June 3

God, life often becomes a ritual—the same routine on a different day. But for Americans, life does not have to be like that. We are free to go about the day in our own way. Please help me stop taking my freedoms for granted and start enjoying the simpler things in life: a walk along a wooded trail, a conversation with a child, a day off to do as I wish and to celebrate my freedoms. Please, God, help me break my day in, day out routine. Help me see there is much more to life as an American. Amen.

☆ ☆ ☆ ☆ ☆

If we forget those who have sacrificed their lives to defend our freedom, we risk forgetting that our freedom is worth dying for in the first place.

June 4

Dear God, sometimes I feel like I live on a swiftly tilting planet with changes swirling around me: changes in relationships and addresses, changes in styles of worship and styles of living, changes in people and causes I trust. Keep me rooted, God, in the one thing that does not change: your love for me, for my country, and for all the world's people. In the whirlwind of my life, please remind me of the security of your unchanging presence and love. Lead me to a quiet place today where I can sit beside the still waters and be renewed by the one constant truth of our world, our nation, and my life. Amen.

June 5

Lord, among the most heartening scenes on television are the images of volunteers, arriving at the site of a tragedy after driving all night, ready to clear wreckage or retrieve bodies.

Our emotions are touched by all the good Samaritans who jump to the aid of their neighbors at disaster scenes ravaged by flood, tornado, hurricane, or fire. How rich we are in America!

Our citizens also volunteer in schools, hospitals, national parks, and museums. Some help with child care, some serve food at shelters, and some build houses.

You have planted your love in their hearts, God. They are your hands in the world. We thank you for a place where so many consider it important to care for their neighbors. We are grateful for our volunteers, our country's most precious resource.

June 6

Thank you for the faith of our fathers and mothers, for generations of faithful folks who worked and prayed and sacrificed to make our country great.

They had faith in each other, and they trusted neighbors and friends who took up arms in defense of freedom. And they had faith in us, that we would do the right thing and preserve the heritage for which they sacrificed. But most of all, they had faith in you—that you would bless their noble work with freedom and enduring joy. They were right. Thank you.

☆　☆　☆　☆　☆

A wise mind knows that adverse events are blessed opportunities for growth in disguise.

June 7

God, with you as our source of all that is good and kind we cannot fail. With your innumerable blessings, both seen and unseen, we lack for nothing. With you as our inner voice we cannot lose our way. With you as our power we cannot be overcome. With you, dear God, we can do all things. With open hearts we are ready to receive your healing, your strength, your infinite love now. And so it is.

☆ ☆ ☆ ☆ ☆

The difficult we do immediately.
The impossible takes a little longer.

United States Army Service Forces motto
during World War II

June 8

O Holy One, we come to you a shattered people. Sorrow weighs us down. We feel surrounded by enemies. We are undone. We see tragedy around us, and we have no energy left to focus on the positive aspects of life. Pressures have built up within and without. We fear we cannot go on. And then we remember that you are not through with the world or with us. We hear a dim echo: With God all things are possible. And we know that the world can be repaired one step at a time if we lift our heads high and take that first step.

Help us not to be overwhelmed by this world's problems. Give us the strength to stand tall and search for solutions, form coalitions, anticipate the possible. Keep these words echoing in our hearts: With God all things are possible. All things are possible with God.

June 9

Dear God, the freedoms we have taken for granted for so long have always been endangered by evil that preys on our weakness and especially on our inattention. Today is no different from any other day since our country was founded. We need prayer to keep your veil of protection over us, and we need it today and in all our days to come. Heavenly Father, help me remember to pray. Touch the hearts of millions so they turn to God in prayer, if just for a moment, every day. Amen.

☆ ☆ ☆ ☆ ☆

Where liberty dwells, there is my country.

Benjamin Franklin, in a letter to B. Vaughan,
March 14, 1783

June 10

Heavenly Father, today I pray for the prisoners of our country. I know that our laws ensure, as far as humanly possible, that justice prevails in our courts and that the punishment fits the crime in humane ways. Those behind bars are paying their debt to society, but let this also be a time for them to turn to you for solace, regret, forgiveness, faith, and renewal. Give them assurance that your mighty love is not kept out by prison guards and prison bars. Let them see that the light of your love can change hearts and lives. Give them hope, Lord, for a better life full of your guidance. Amen.

☆ ☆ ☆ ☆ ☆

It is difficult to hate those you pray for; you begin to feel responsible for them. They become part of your family.

June 11

Americans share the most precious gift: freedom. That means we are free to stand up for one another, protect one another, and love one another. Please, God, help those who see evil all  around also see the good in their fellow Americans.

Make America the home of the compassionate and caring. Help us to forget our trivial flaws and love one another simply because we are all Americans. Amen.

June 12

Dear God, it's vacation time now, and people are traveling. The streets and highways and interstates are full of cars. The sky is crowded with planes. People are getting on trains and buses for business and visits and family adventures. Thank you, God, for the freedom we have in America to travel with so few restrictions.

I ask for safety for all those travelers. Please help the planes take off and land without incident. Help the cars and trucks and buses operate properly. Help tired drivers stay awake and focus on the road. Help moms and dads keep their children buckled up and strapped in. Please bless this nation with safe travel. Amen.

June 13

God of the ages, we thank you for all things. Today we give special thanks for our flag, our country's symbol. We wave it high; we wave it proudly.

Our flag is not just sentiment— it represents our country's proud history. It reminds us of the experiences of our people in good times and bad.

You have been the major portion of our history, Lord. You have been our refuge, our strength, our help, and our hope throughout the ages. Stand by us now as we pray, as we raise our flags, for with these banners we honor you, our God, as well as our country.

June 14
Flag Day

Our Father, I pray to you today to thank you for "Old Glory."
We proudly display the emblem of our country above our
rolling lands and shimmering seas. The American flag tells
stories of days past. It's a national tribute to all its defenders
who lost their lives. Thank you, Lord, for our Star-Spangled
Banner. May it forever wave over our nation as a symbol of the
free and a sign of the brave. Amen.

☆ ☆ ☆ ☆ ☆

Break out the flag, strike up the band, light up the sky.
President Gerald R. Ford, National Proclamation, July 1976

June 15

Summer is coming to America, Lord, bringing with it blue-and-white dappled skies and warm winds that whisper across the forests, plains, and mountains. Life is lighter, brighter, friendlier in the lazy heat that lies on the beaches and fields. It seems easier, somehow, to go out and *be*—just *live,* without intent.

And that's what you told us to do, isn't it? Live for the day, like the lilies of the field. Just be what we are, as we are. Just live.

Walking with you is like eternal summer. We bask in your love as we do in the warmth and light of the sun. We feel the touch of your voice as we do the summer breeze. We can be as we are and know that what we are is good in your eyes.

June 16

The people of our country are known to be among the friend-
iest in the world. The glory goes to you, Father, for you have
given us contentment and taught us to love one another. Con-
inue to shape us and mold us in your image.

Help us to value each of our neighbors and to treat them with
respect and genuine affection. When we forget, call us back
and remind us again with your love.

Through the friendly spirit of our people, may we continue to
demonstrate to others our joy in your presence.

☆　☆　☆　☆　☆

To be American is to be blessed.

June 17

Lord, from coast to coast the children have come home from school. Lives change when the children come home. Things seem a little less organized, a little less manageable, a little less calm. Of course, things also seem a little more energetic, a little more exciting, a little more lively. Help all of us, whether or not we have children of our own, to welcome the kids home with open arms. Help us love them, encourage them, guide and direct them, accept them. Help us not to get exasperated, irritated, uptight, or unloving. No matter whose children they are, they hold the future in their hands. Help all adults to view all children as you do— precious, wondrous, and amazing. The children are home, God . . . give us strength. Amen.

June 18

God of Peace,

help us to know the things that make for peace.

May our everyday actions with friends and strangers
    lead to peace.

May the work we do with our hands lead to peace.

May our thoughts focus on possibilities of peace.

May the policies of our government work toward peace.

Keep our hearts hungry for peace.

Encourage us in all we do as individuals and as a nation,
    that peace might one day reign on earth.

Let there be peace . . .
    and let it begin with us.

Amen.

June 19

Lord, please make us aware of people in our country who live oppressed lives. Sometimes we forget that not everyone in America has a free and blessed life. Some are oppressed because of their ethnic heritage. Some because of their economic status. Some because of their educational background. Some because of physical or mental disabilities. Some because of their religious beliefs.

Whatever the reasons are, God, no one should live under oppressive circumstances, especially in this land that promotes freedom. If we are personally guilty of oppressing either an individual or a group of people, forgive us. Point out our failure, and help us change our attitudes and behaviors so that we are accepting of everyone. Open our hearts so that we learn to love all people. Amen.

June 20

As our Father, you know how essential dads are. Children need a daddy who not only provides for them but also loves them and gives wise direction to their lives. Lord, you know how many families in our nation are missing fathers. Death, divorce, and misaligned priorities steal men away from their families.

I ask that you would turn the hearts of the fathers toward their children. Please remind them of their responsibility. Help them see the great opportunity to make their families strong.

And for the fathers who have accepted their noble duty, Lord, I ask you to give them strength. Grant them wisdom to know how to instill strong values in their kids. Grant them patience. And grant them the ability to communicate love and acceptance. God, make America's fathers strong and loving.

June 21

As Americans, we are stirred by the words from our Declaration of Independence, "We hold these truths to be self-evident: that all men are created equal...."

How comforting to remember that you, Lord, our Creator, have bestowed on us the right to life, liberty, and the pursuit of happiness. When people tried to take those rights away, it took a government of the people to make them secure.

Keep that government strong, O God, against powers that would try to bring it to its knees. With you on our side, Lord, we shall continue to be "the land of the free and the home of the brave."

June 22

Holy God, I beseech you to speak to the heart of America and teach us perspective. We have floods but no famine. We have drought but no thirst. We have crime but no anarchy. We have problems, but we have wisdom and systems to solve them. And we have faith, the cornerstone of our country, that withstands every storm. In your name, amen.

☆ ☆ ☆ ☆ ☆

Like the lighthouse beacon, faith guides our way through the fog of fear, doubt, and uncertainty to the sea of clarity beyond.

June 23

God, you have blessed this nation with a depth and width of
variety that is nearly incomprehensible:
trees with leaves, palms, and needles
weather from warm to cold, rainy to dry, windy to calm
water that is fresh and water that is salty
birds that swim and birds that fly
wildlife that runs, creeps, slinks, and slithers
mountains that soar, hills that rise, plains that stretch, valleys
    that dip, and canyons that descend
clouds that are fingered, puffed, dotted, and dispersed
people that are tall and short, dark and light, young and old.

Our land is filled with every shape, every size, every color,
every texture, every this, and every that. What a glorious gift
you've given us, God. Thank you. Amen.

June 24

What is an American, Lord? An American is one who has pride in their country, a person who stands up for what he or she believes in. An American has understanding and helpful words for those around them. An American is not afraid to be different. An American is free. An American cares for his  brothers and sisters. An American does not discriminate. An American does not back down when challenged. An American stands behind fellow Americans in times of need. An American, God, is all these things and more. Amen.

June 25

Today, Father, be with every child in America who has no parents. Wrap your strong, loving, and gentle arms around their bodies and souls. Reassure them of your love. Whisper encouragement to their souls. Hold them safely in the harbor of your presence. God, bring forward the adults who can fill the roles of mother and father to these children. Give those adults courage, strength, vision, and guidance. Shower them with blessings and hope. Give them deep reservoirs of love for children who desperately need it. Bring healing and comfort to those children who have been broken or harmed. Bring hope to those children who feel hopeless. Bring welcoming acceptance to those children who have been rejected. No child should be alone, especially in a land that is blessed as richly and abundantly as ours. Bless the children, God, and show each of us what you would have us do to give them a future. Amen.

June 26

Dear God, we want to be a generous people. We have seen fellow Americans ride hundreds of miles to raise money for AIDS research, donate tons of food to the hungry, cross oceans to help those hit by natural disasters. We are cheered by the child who empties her piggy bank to give to the homeless family, and we honor the grandfather who walks three days for a cancer fundraiser.

Help us continue to live in that generous spirit. Inspire us to think more about others' needs than our own busy schedules or strained budgets. Remind us that to live in this country is to have access to resources few in the world have. Nudge each of us to discover our gifts for giving, that we may extend your love into our world. Help us know when to put our needs second. Remind us of the joy we find in reaching out to those in need. Help us to be a generous people. Amen.

June 27

Thank you, God, for these lazy, hazy days of summer. For barbecue cookouts and pool parties with friends and neighbors; for Fourth of July fireworks and baseball games and hot dogs; for visits to theme parks and Little League; for stargazing on balmy nights; for soft night breezes and crickets and ladybugs and grasshoppers; for the feeling of the  warm sun on bare skin; for a refreshing cold drink on a hot summer night; for outdoor concerts and birthday parties and county fairs. Thank you, God. Summertime in America is a great time of year.

June 28

Lord, we celebrate our love for you and for our country. In your steadfast love, you made yourself known to the pilgrims when they braved a harsh new land in the dead of winter.

You guided the writers of the Declaration of Independence, the Constitution, and the Bill of Rights as they put into words the yearnings of people longing to be free.

You directed George Washington as he learned on the job to define the duties of a president in a democracy.

You have been present as each leader made his mark on our country and as each citizen learned the meaning of freedom.

You have blessed our land, Lord God, and filled our hearts with love and thanksgiving.

June 29

Everyone has ideas about the right and wrong way to live: society, our parents, our partners, and even us. The trouble is, ideas differ, and in the end we get confused and ask, "What should I do?"

Often the result is a compromise. Tolerance and give and take are valuable qualities. No society and no friendship will function without them. But what if it all turns sour?

We've all made poor bargains from time to time, accepted someone else's values only to find they weren't doing us good.

Lord, when we're asked to compromise, help us decide if it's what you would want. Let's talk to find out if it's good, if it's true, and if it will make our lives better. And if the answer is yes, let us embrace our choices knowing they are your will.

June 30

Dear Lord,
Everything looks much
    brighter than it did before.
Our nation's prayer for strength
    has been answered.
Our cries for help have been
    heard.
Our pleas for mercy flew directly
    to your throne.
Now we're ready to help
    our neighbors, Lord.
Let us not delay.

July 1

The American flag boasts fifty stars. Fifty points of light standing side by side. Lord God, you have shown us how we, as states, become more than the sum of our parts as we stand together. Individually, we are tiny parcels of territory with limited resources and tremendous vulnerabilities. Together, we are a force to be reckoned with, the greatest nation on the face of the earth. And I am so proud, Father, that we have chosen to stand together for ideals that honor you: liberty, freedom, peace, justice. Let the light of these fifty stars keep shining strong, bright, and united in you. Amen.

☆ ☆ ☆ ☆ ☆

God ignites the stars upon our nation's flag, keeping them shining through sunny celebrations; farewells to heroes; and our long, dark nights.

July 2

Father, it is justice that makes democracy possible in our great country. When others wrong us, a cry goes up for a swift accounting of justice.

We rely on you, Lord, to help us react in fairness and reason. We need you to help us understand the true meaning of justice.

You are a God of justice, and you require it of your children. Be our model now as we strive to do your will and be your witnesses in the world.

The cry for liberty rises in every human soul. How fortunate we are to live in a land where that cry is met with a wide open door of freedom and opportunity.

July 3

God, I recall from my youth many Fourth of July parades and fireworks. I loved celebrating Independence Day because of all the festivities. But now that I'm older, Lord, I love the festivities because they are a memorial to an amazing triumph of vision and courage. Thank you for those men and women of the eighteenth century who risked their personal safety, even spilling their blood, to forge this nation. Thank you for their strong and brave character. Help me today, Father, as I continue in their footsteps, doing my part to keep the light of liberty shining brightly.

July 4
Independence Day

Today is the birthday of my country, God. I give thanks and praise for its noble beginnings, its unwavering founders, and the bravery of all who have fought to sustain it. May the red, white, and blue banner of the free continue to wave high above our land. I ask you, Lord, to keep it free from hatred and protect it from harm. Amen.

☆ ☆ ☆ ☆ ☆

The United States themselves are essentially the greatest poem.

Walt Whitman, *Leaves of Grass*

Statue of Liberty

July 5

Dear God, I know this land isn't my final home. I know I'll spend forever in heaven with you. And that's my greatest hope and closest comfort. But, Father, I love this country you've placed me in. I love the expanse of it. I love the diversity of it. And, mostly, I love the freedom you've given us in it.

I know that one day I'll dwell in a land flowing with milk and honey, where I'll roam golden streets with dry eyes and perfect peace. In the meantime, though, I'm so grateful to live in the land of the free and home of the brave, where I'm free to speak your name and enjoy your blessings.

July 6

Lord, in times of trouble, you shine like a light in the darkness. Your love is a beacon that shows us where to walk. Your word is a comfort to us and a guide through uncertain times.

Give us your blessing as we go out into this day. Let us take your light out into our world to share with people less fortunate than we are. Let your light shine through us to bring comfort to people burdened with sadness. Let your light shine through us to bring your promise of eternal glory to those without hope. Let your light shine through us to show your truth to everyone we meet.

Let us carry a spark of divine light into our world today.

July 7

The fields that feed our young and old
stretch from east to west, north to south,
blanketing the prairies, cloaking the valleys,
gently draping the hills.
The patchwork of brown and black,
greens and golds sway in the breeze,
bend in the wind, reach toward the sun.
Down into the earth, roots drink deeply
from the soil's richness and the land's wealth.
Thank you, Father, for the food you give
and for the ground from which it grows.

July 8

Heavenly Father, you made us in your image. For that we are proud and honored. Help us as individuals and as Americans to fulfill the hopes you place in us. Guide us so we can find a way to live according to the laws you have given us.

We belong to many families: the family of our earthly parents, the family of Americans, and the family of the world. Most of all, Lord, remind us that we are all part of your family: children of one God.

☆　☆　☆　☆　☆

America is a patchwork quilt of many colors, shapes, and patterns, stitched together with the threads of common experience.

July 9

The earth and everything in it is yours, Lord. We thank you for sharing our beautiful country with us. We are only stewards.

How can we properly show our appreciation for the oceans and mountains, the lakes and prairies, the forests and coastlines that make up our homeland?

We love our country, Father, and hold it dear. Bless our land and our people, and bind us ever closer to you.

☆　☆　☆　☆　☆

Ask an American to sit down and count his or her blessings, and you will be there awhile. No other country on earth offers such abundant opportunities and ample natural wonders as these United States.

July 10

Turn my heart toward the people around me, Lord. They are my fellow Americans. Help me seek friendship in their faces. Keep me from the kind of indifference and fear that assumes the worst about them. Instead, help me give the benefit of the doubt whenever I can, believe the best about their intentions, and seek out and find the good in them. I want to value my country by valuing its precious citizens.

★ ★ ★ ★ ☆

Our differences inspire us.
Our commonalities unite us.
Our dreams empower us.
Our hopes encourage us.

July 11

Father, I'd given up on the idea of heroes. As I got older, the sports stars, actors, and politicians I admired all turned out to be so human, so frail, so ordinary. *Why do I need heroes,* I wondered. *People are just people.*

But lately I've started noticing men and women who are different. They sacrifice themselves for others. When crisis hits, they show up. They give more than I thought humans had in them to get the job done. And they do it all by serving their country—this country—in police and fire departments, in hospitals, and in the military.

God, thank you for these new heroes. Thank you for preparing them for this moment and placing them where we need them. And thank you for helping me understand what a real hero is—a person willing to sacrifice for their brothers and sisters.

July 12

Father God, in you we trust our lives and freedom. Let me linger for a moment and, with your guiding hand, see a sacrifice I can make to extend our nation's bounty to other lands. Your love for humankind is a gift so grand I sometimes fail to understand that to completely unwrap this gift I must share it, in your name, beyond my country's borders with suffering people whose names I will never know. Amen.

☆　☆　☆　☆　☆

Love is an active force. When we "walk our talk" and live God's message of love, we create an America full of faith. When we do that, we are God's voice, his hands, his light for each other. We are living love.

July 13

God, today I need to pray for something other than myself. I need to pray for America and its citizens. May they always form a chain of belief and faith in the institution of our country. War can be waged on us, but we will not cower. We will stand proud and strong—stronger than we were before. So I ask you, God, to help us keep our faith and belief in America, its leaders, and its citizens. Amen.

☆ ☆ ☆ ☆ ☆

A nation is a reflection of its people: America the beautiful.

July 14

God, I am refreshed and renewed today after sleeping in the security of your love. But I also had the blessing of sleeping in a country where people guard my community, state, and nation. God bless these guardians with every grace; bless each police officer, firefighter, soldier, and sailor. Their names are seldom mentioned in newspapers or on

TV, but they do a hero's work every day. As they prepare for sleep this evening, please touch them with your soothing hand so that they, too, may sleep in peace.

July 15

Lord, it's good to know that our prayers don't need to be lofty and grand. We just need to speak from our hearts.

We Americans value friendship, Lord. How else could we have made our country what it is, if not by sticking together and helping each other? Thank you for friends. Help us be good friends to everyone we know and love.

We value freedom and independence. Thank you, Lord, for our right to choose. Guide us in making the right choices.

We value our work, and we work hard for what we have. Thank you for the strength to support ourselves and our families.

Friendship, freedom, and rightful pride may be homely virtues, Lord, but they come from our hearts.

July 16

Father, this is the month in which we celebrate our freedom. We set off fireworks into the night sky. We gather with family and eat outside. We wave flags and listen to patriotic music. It's our way of remembering the great freedom you've given us in America.

Thank you, God, for these traditions. Thanks for the fireworks and the cookouts and the parades, all of which remind us to tell our children why we love this country so much and why they should, too. Thank you mostly for that very freedom we celebrate. Help us never forget what it cost and what it's worth.

☆ ☆ ☆ ☆ ☆

America is not only a wonderful place to visit,
it is the best place to live.

July 17

(Based on Isaiah 43)

Loving God, in times of trouble all we can do is rest on your promises. Help us remember your promise to be with us:

> Do not fear, for I have redeemed you:
> I have called you by name, you are mine.
> When you pass through the waters, I will be with you;
> and through the rivers, they shall not overwhelm you.
> For I am the Lord your God,
> the Holy One of Israel, your Savior...
> You are precious in my sight,
> and honored, and I love you.

Strengthen us so that we know that you will take care of us. Help us cast our worries on you. We need to feel your loving arms wrapped around us. We are your faithful people. Amen.

July 18

God, without a vision, we will fall apart as a country. Without a vision, we will live meaningless lives. Without a vision, we will have no reason to wake up each morning and start a new day. God, please give us a vision. Give us a vision of what this country can do and can become. Don't let us be satisfied with "average" or "acceptable." Don't let us sit back complacently, resting on our past, relying on it to propel us forward.

We want to be people of purpose, people of substance, and people of character. We want to do more than go through the motions or follow a shallow checklist. We want to have a vision, as a country and as individuals. Give each of us a vision that, when combined with all the others, becomes a focus of direction and hope. Without a vision people will perish. You alone can give us this vision. Amen.

July 19

Father, thank you for the "grandparents" of this nation—the praiseworthy men and women of the past who have invested their lives in making this a great country. I owe them a debt of gratitude, dear Lord, and I pause to honor them now. I thank you for their dedication to the welfare of the USA. I bless them for their love of country and commitment to making it an even better place for those who would come after them. I pause for a moment of silence in memory of those who have given their lives to that end. Amen.

☆ ☆ ☆ ☆ ☆

A chosen country, with room enough for our descendants to the thousandth and thousandth generation.

President Thomas Jefferson, Inaugural Address, 1801

July 20

The warm sunshine on my back, God, is reassurance that you are watching. The warm summer breeze whispers your words of guidance. Never is your presence more easily felt than in the changing of the seasons. It's comforting to know that even though every day brings elements that may be unexpected, the sun will rise and set, and the seasons will change. You are a mighty God. Amen.

☆ ☆ ☆ ☆ ☆

*Faith is never proven through logic or reason;
it must be felt with the heart.*

July 21

Lord, the decisions my country's leaders make today will be tomorrow's reality. Their laws and regulations, their every act, are stones thrown into an ocean that ripples to every shore. God, bless our leaders and guide them in every decision, no matter how small. Let my prayers and the prayers of others fill them with wisdom and foresight. Each one was elected in trust. Help them honor our trust, hold firm to our faith in them, and look to you as the final judge of what is good and right and true. Amen.

U.S. Capitol Building

July 22

Lord, as our country grew, we asked for pleasure, and you gave us hard work. We asked for happiness, and you gave us grief. We asked for success, and you gave us struggle.

We did not understand then that these were your gifts to us. For without hard work, we would not know the pleasure of leisure. Without struggle, we would not appreciate success. Without grief, we would not understand how priceless happiness is.

In your wisdom you have given us what we need in order to achieve the things we desire. In so doing, you have made us stronger. How wonderful are your ways in all the earth!

July 23

Turn our hearts toward you, O God! Help us as a nation to realize that you are our source of comfort and strength, not only in crisis but also in prosperity. Keep us from attitudes of pride and self-sufficiency that would cause us to ignore you. Grant us humility that we may continue to experience your great grace and blessing. Amen.

★ ★ ★ ★ ★

An optimistic outlook may not speed your journey,
but it does improve the scenery along the way.

July 24

Heavenly Father, every day I can set aside a bit of my time and resources to share—but where? I'm torn between Greenpeace and world peace, Save the Children and Save the Whales, the Girl Scouts and the Red Cross. Should I spend an hour in prayer or an hour with a friend in need? Should I pray for my country, pray for my neighbor, or pray for a refugee? God, in your wisdom, please guide me today to serve with my hands and my prayers where I am most needed. Amen.

☆ ☆ ☆ ☆ ☆

Inspiration is the alignment of our talents with God's purpose.

July 25

God, the faces of our children are fresh with wonder and excitement and awe. They see the world through eyes of hope, with hearts of joy. They breathe in the sun. They drink in the sky. They soak up the earth. They dance in the wind, giggle at bugs, and applaud the stars. Help us to be like them.

The faces of our elderly are lined with love and life and peace. They see the world through eyes of wisdom, with hearts of courage. They meditate on truth. They rejoice in commitment. They reflect on character. They dance in the breeze, smile at new life, and applaud the heavens above. Help us to be like them. Amen.

July 26

Lord, Americans are resourceful and gifted. We can create beauty using skillful hands and thoughtful minds. Our creativity helps us make the world a better place. Let our works reflect, in some small way, your glorious act of creation.

We don't all have fine words to pray, Lord. But let us remember that the word "inspiration" comes from "spirit"; let others accept the gifts of our creation and prayers. A simple home-baked loaf of bread, a heartfelt poem, or a blanket sewn for a baby's bed all speak of the same time, love, and devotion as does a wordy prayer.

Help us encourage our children to be creators. Those who draw from the well of creation within themselves are less inclined to destroy. Guide our hands, hearts, and thoughts as we help you make our country a more lovely place for all of us.

July 27

Lord, you promised to send the seasons as long as the earth endures. It
is reassuring to know you have not
failed us and that summer has
arrived according to your timetable.

We anticipate vacations and the
easing of schedules—time out to
renew body and soul. We look for-
ward to the yield of the earth—succulent fruits and vegetables,
grains, and brilliant flowers crowned with color and fragrance.

Our fertile homeland is a refreshing garden, full of beauty and
nourishment. May it continue to bear good fruit in your name,
O Lord.

July 28

Good morning, God. I have a special need today. You have called us to be people of salt and light. I confess I miss so many opportunities as I go about my day focused on my "to do" list and my personal concerns. Help me, Lord, to share the light of your love with a word or a smile or a helpful act today. Help me season this day with one of the many manifestations of your presence. Lord, I have no excuse for omitting "salt" and "light" from my daily list. In thanksgiving for your great gifts, the least I can do is sprinkle a little salt, shed a little light. With your help and by your grace, I shall. In your name I pray, amen.

July 29

Father, it's not always easy to maintain a good attitude toward those you've placed in authority over us. From the president to our local city council, our nature is to second-guess and criticize. That's not always a bad thing, Father, but I ask that you

help us respect and support our nation's leaders—even when we disagree with them.

According to your word, Father, those authorities are there because you want them there. Even those opposed to you are working out your will for America. Help us honor you by following our leaders wisely. And please, Father, put honorable men and women into those leadership roles.

July 30

How fortunate we are, Lord, to have a network of roads and highways connecting the sections of our country from north to south and east to west. We can travel freely wherever we choose throughout the land, without permissions or passports.

What freedom we enjoy and what choices!

We are bound together not only by roads but by a spirit of unity. In you, Heavenly Father, there is no east or west, north or south. You make us all one. Thank you for this fellowship. Help us to strengthen and protect this precious connection.

July 31

America is such a beautiful land. We talk of amber waves of grain and purple mountains majesty, but that is just a quick assessment. America is beautiful in every way. Of course its landscapes are beautiful but so are its people, its beliefs, its freedoms, its leaders, and its history. I am so thankful to be a part of America and so proud to call it home. Amen.

☆ ☆ ☆ ☆ ☆

Gratitude must guard the American soul. Without it, we will become reckless, foolish, and greedy. With it, however, we remain peaceful, contented, and generous—a people who can afford to be proud.

August 1

A place to rest. A place to find solace. A place to rejuvenate. A place to soak in the beauty of nature. God, thank you for this great wide country that affords so many places to find what my soul is hungry for. Grant me, in the heart of these summer days, time to find such a place, even if it's in my own backyard. Help me stop to catch my breath, touch base with you, and revel in the pleasure of relaxation in the land of the free.

★　★　★　★　☆

The strongest weapon that any nation has is simply this: love and respect for all humankind.

August 2

Every day, people walk the beaches, leaving winding trails of footprints in the sand. And every day without fail, you cause the waves to wash ashore and smooth the signs away, taking all traces of turmoil with them as the water swirls and eddies back into the ocean. What remains are ripples in the damp sand, as though you, Lord, had signed your work for us to see.

Maybe praying is like that. Maybe spending a little time with you once or twice a day can help smooth over the troubles in our lives and wash away the turmoil. Maybe if we take time to listen, we'll hear your voice as you speak, feel your love more deeply, see your signs more clearly.

Lord, help us make the time to draw close to you in prayer so you can smooth the sands of our lives.

August 3

Help us to put our trust in you, O God. We see that the things of this world do not sustain us. When trouble comes we are like saplings swaying in the wind, and we fear our roots are not strong enough to hold us firm. Let us be rooted in your love and nourished by your constant presence, that we might stand tall even when adversity threatens to tear us apart. As you have been with humanity throughout the eons, stay by us now and help us be worthy of your love and care. Amen.

☆ ☆ ☆ ☆ ☆

Great faith is not found; it is made of tiny demonstrations of commitment on a daily basis.

August 4

Gracious God, you have called your people to peace, and we have failed generation after generation. Our great country was founded on the blood of patriots and the blood of British soldiers that, in the end, were vanquished. Since then, we have fought other countries and even fought among ourselves in your name and for your glory. Lord, I know that freedom and human rights must be defended. Yet you call us to peace. Help me, Lord, to live in peace with my neighbors. Give me hope that one day all your people will pray, "God, make me an instrument of your peace." On that day the bloodshed will stop. Amen.

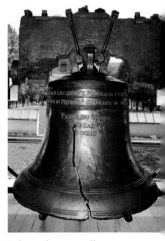

The Liberty Bell

August 5

Seeking courage, Lord, our country bundles its fears and
      places them in your hands.
Too heavy for us, too weighty even to ponder in
      this moment,
such shadowy terrors shrink in our minds
      and—how wonderful!—
wither to nothing in your grasp.

      ★   ★   ★   ★   ☆

Hope steadies the faltering soul.

August 6

Lord, thank you for the amazing beauty of this land we live in. Your creation is magnificent. It leaves us speechless, whether we are standing near the edge of the Grand Canyon, walking through sequoia forests, splashing in the ocean, or climbing the southern hills. There are miracles of nature surrounding us on all sides. We are blessed with the magnitude, the breadth, the variety, and the fullness of all you have made. Help us each gain a new appreciation for the beauty that defines our own homes, even as we learn to appreciate the beauty that defines the faraway places of our country. We are blessed beyond imagination, Lord, and for this we thank you. Amen.

August 7

Lord, help us be people who matter. Not rock stars and movie icons, millionaires and marathon winners. No, Lord, help us be really important people. The kind of people who help in times of need. The kind of people who appreciate others and make them feel special. The kind of people who teach children to tie their shoelaces, ride a bike, or catch crayfish in a stream. You know, the really important things in life.

The people who count in life, Lord, are the everyday heroes who show us how to live and love: grandparents, friends, teachers, and neighbors who shape our lives and share their time, their love, and themselves with us.

Show us what we can do today to change our world for the better and be people who count.

August 8

It is not always easy to live up to the title of "American." I must not separate individuals because they are not of my race or do not practice my religion. I must not single out others because they are different. I must not slander others' names because they do not believe what I believe. For they are as American as I am. They are free, just as I am free. Amen.

☆　☆　☆　☆　☆

This nation's greatest asset is the multicolored, richly textured, intricately woven tapestry made up of countless individual Americans.

August 9

Dear God, please help me have a Sunday kind of Monday, glad to awaken to another week of work. I want to carry through on Sunday's prayers—my prayers and the prayers of people across the country, in places of worship large and small, of every denomination and faith. On Sunday, we praise you, we ask for help, and we make promises. Now it is Monday, and I do not want to forget those things that bring me close to you. Help

me praise you, seek your help, search for your face in everyone I meet, and keep my promises today and throughout the week. Amen.

August 10

Father, you've allowed us to become one of the richest nations ever. Compared to the rest of the world, very few of us lack food, shelter, or clothing. In fact, most of us live in what the rest of this globe would describe as luxury. Houses. Cars. Clothes. Electronics. Convenience. We live in great bounty.

Thank you, Lord, for those innumerable blessings. Thank you for meeting our needs and giving us so much that we can scarcely enjoy it all. Help us never forget that every good gift comes from you. And help us overcome our tendency to trust those things instead of you.

August 11

We see your love, O God, reflected across the spacious skies of our great nation. Your power is known in purple mountain majesties, and your abundant gifts to us are apparent in amber waves

of grain. Yet even as we give thanks for your many gifts to us, we know that in every nation, in every individual heart, you work for good. Your gracious care extends past national boundary lines, crosses the divide of diverse languages, and rests on all your children. Help us find ways to learn about other nations, other citizens and their lives, so that we may join together across all boundaries and walls to work with you for the good of our world and all its people. Amen.

August 12

Dear God, thank you for the countless gifts and abilities you've given to the people of this country. Thank you for the mathematicians, the electricians, the artists, the teachers, the caretakers, the builders, and everyone in between. For those who cannot make sense of their checkbooks, bankers are miraculous. For those who cannot hit a nail on the head, builders are phenomenal. For those who cannot discern "on" from "off," electricians are the salt of the earth.

Truly, God, you have given to all of us something that we can give back to others. Help us see others through new eyes, no longer viewing and labeling them by their occupation but rather recognizing and affirming their abilities and talents. Amen.

August 13

In these lazy days of summer may we refresh our spirits. Let this be a season of connecting with friends, spending time outdoors, taking time to appreciate the beauty of nature in all its fullness. And as we relax into a summer routine, inspire us to do at least one random act of kindness each day, that the world might know your love through us. Amen.

☆ ☆ ☆ ☆ ☆

America's greatest strength is her people, both as individuals and as members of a community.

August 14

Dear God, thank you for the land you have entrusted to us, for the glory of flowers, wild creatures, and trees. Help us conserve our bountiful resources of rich soil and clean water. Help us remember to protect the birds that ask nothing of us but that we let them sing. You give us the beauty and solace of nature. Let us understand that to cover our country with concrete is to blind ourselves to beauty and deafen ourselves to the earth's soothing music. Amen.

★ ★ ★ ★ ☆

Between her two shining seas, America is an ocean of people who shine brighter than all the seas and stars combined.

August 15

Lord, we know change is inevitable. Teach our country to accept it. If we view each transition as an opportunity to experience your faithfulness, then we make new places in our lives for spiritual growth. Thank you.

☆ ☆ ☆ ☆ ☆

God is our refuge and strength, a very present help in trouble. Therefore we will not fear, though the earth should change, though the mountains shake in the heart of the sea; though its waters roar and foam, though the mountains tremble with its tumult.
The Lord of hosts is with us.

Psalm 46:1–3, 7

August 16

Almighty and merciful God, pour out your spirit on this nation that we may faithfully serve you and all your children. Keep us constant, give us compassion, help us to live with integrity. Guide and direct us so that each of us, no matter what we call you or how we understand you, may live steadfast to your call. In your great name we pray, amen.

☆ ☆ ☆ ☆ ☆

Freedom without boundaries is not freedom at all, but rather chaos and confusion.

August 17

I thank you, Lord, for airports and train stations filled with hugs and hope. I sit and watch the multi-cultural crowd, alive with energy, anxiety, vitality, and joy.

We are a people on the move. We have waited for the ship and stage and train to take us west and bring us home. And by your grace, we find our purpose and our place.

Thank you for this simple freedom—the freedom to decide where we want to go and the ability to go there. Give us grace, and bring us safely home. Amen.

August 18

Help us, God, to heal and rebuild when we are hurt. Help us to forgive and forget when we are wrong. Help us to console and comfort when we are sad. Help us to be one and stand tall when we are afraid. Help us to live and be proud because we are Americans. Amen.

★ ★ ★ ★ ★

Living the American dream doesn't mean we don't have to act. It means we plan, we act, and then we trust in God to help us reach our goals.

August 19

When we doubt your miracle-making power, Lord, show us the ordinary miracles of season, of hope regained, of love from family and friends, of civil decency, of humility, and of surprises that turn out to be miracles that remake our lives.

The one thing this country needs, above all other things, in its effort to thrive is this: knees bent in humble adoration while individuals fervently pray to God Almighty.

August 20

Blessed Father, comfort our nation's citizens today. Remind us of your steadfast love and concern for us and that you will never forsake us. Give us wisdom to understand that your ways are not our ways nor are your thoughts our thoughts, and that there is a time and a purpose for everything under heaven. We turn to you in faith, Good Father, knowing that you will keep watch over your flock.

☆ ☆ ☆ ☆ ☆

We never outgrow our need for faith. No one is too strong, too mature, or too experienced to benefit from its grace.

August 21

Some prayers are best left unfinished, God of abundance, and this will be an ongoing conversation between us. Each day, I discover new gifts you offer me and my country, and the list of reasons to be thankful grows. As I accept your gifts and live with them thankfully, guide me and other Americans to become people who share with others, here and around the world, so that they, too, can live abundantly. May someone, somewhere, someday say of us, "I am truly thankful to have these people in my life."

★　★　★　★　☆

*Take time to reflect on the people and things around you.
It is in these quiet moments that inspiration grows
and we recognize the miracle of life.*

August 22

Father, today we pray for the leaders of our country.
Please, God, grant them

> humility as they fill the role of civil servant,
> integrity as they represent the people of their
> constituencies,
> honesty as they deal with other leaders,
> wisdom as they make decisions,
> compassion as they work for citizens with critical needs,
> vision as they look ahead to what this country can be
> and can do.

God, we know their jobs are difficult. We know they face tough decisions on a regular basis. Protect their minds, their hearts, and their souls. Thank you for the role they play in this country. Guide them in the direction that will prove best for everyone. Amen.

August 23

There is no God like our God.
Righteousness and justice form the foundation
    of God's throne.
God's goodness is known throughout the earth.
The love of God is unfathomable.
We sing your praises.
There is no God like our God!

☆ ☆ ☆ ☆ ☆

Let us live today so that when future generations look back
on our lives they say respectfully, "They lived generous
lives dedicated to the good of their nation."

August 24

God, give us the gift of compassion, that we may know how it feels to walk in another's shoes. Give us the gift of tolerance, that we may accept those who are different even if we do not understand those differences. Give us the gift of hope, that we may look beyond the dark nights of pain and suffering to the dawn of a new tomorrow. Give us the gift of understanding, that we may know our sacred place in the world and use it for the good of all humankind. Amen.

August 25

We thank you for the doctors, nurses, and technicians who help make our bodies strong and well. Give them the wisdom and the skill to do your work. We are grateful for the health care that we have now that keeps us well, and we are grateful for the health care that we may need in the future.

As the Great Physician, give us the cures we lack and the compassion we need. And when we fail, help us to turn to you, the God who heals. Amen.

★ ★ ★ ★ ☆

Hopeful eyes perceive the light where other eyes see only night.

August 26

Heavenly Father, help our nation protect those who are unable to defend themselves, guide our children so they do not lose their way, give hope to those in despair, and offer liberty to people enslaved by sin. Remind us that *we* are the people and that we each must do our part—or our prayers will be small bandages to large wounds and broken hearts. Amen.

★ ★ ★ ★ ★

To help another is not simply kindhearted—it's American.

August 27

When I sit on the porch with a glass of iced tea and look out across the freshly mowed grass, I am thankful for the small pleasure of a job well done. Part of what makes our country

great are those small and common jobs we do with satisfaction and with joy.

Make this my offering to you today, Lord. Give me some small things to do, and make me glad to do them. Help me to do them well and to add to the grand total of a great nation, a nation where work is a privilege and workmanship is a source of pride. Amen.

August 28

God, as Americans, help us be aware of and respect other people and other nations. It is easy to focus only on ourselves and to forget that we are only one part of a larger world. Don't let us become self-serving and prideful. Don't let us fall into the trap of superiority. Help us realize that the rest of the world does not need to be like us.

America represents so much that is good—freedom, liberty, creativity, and individuality. Help us realize, however, that other countries and other people also represent many good things. Help us respect other lands, not look down on them. Help us be thankful for our national identity without thinking we must transfer it onto all other nations. Help us not to become a self-centered people incapable of seeing the world beyond our borders. Amen.

August 29

God, let us mount up on wings of eagles and transcend the suffering of our nation. With hope and faith to guide us, let us fly to a heavenly place where peace, love, and fellowship prevail. Like the majestic hawk that soars above the earth, let us rise to any challenge put before us. Bless our nation, O Lord, and make us stronger still.

☆ ☆ ☆ ☆ ☆

The answer to senseless destruction is purposeful creation.
Art, in all its forms, is a great healer.
If you can write, write.
If you paint, paint.
If you're a potter, turn pots.
You are a child of God, so fill your life with creation.

August 30

You are our strength, O Lord, and so we ask for a measure of your courage when we feel timid, frightened, and overcome by the chaos in the world. Be our Rock and our Redeemer, and fill us with your power so we can face whatever is to come in our lives and our world. Amen.

★ ★ ★ ★ ★

*Hope knows that in the midst of feeling all alone,
God is still with us.*

August 31

Father, I can feel summer loosening its grip. Children are getting ready to go back to school. I know they'll soon be sitting in classrooms, some resisting, some engaging in the process of learning. And I know their teachers will be put to the test to excite their minds with knowledge.

Please, Father, help those teachers succeed in breaking through short attention spans and late nights and missed meals and too much TV and the normal frenzy of childhood. America's future depends on those children learning math and science and history. Give those teachers the strength, courage, and wisdom to teach what's right in the best way possible. And help those children learn, Father, even if it is in spite of themselves.

September 1

Thank you, God, for the work of our hands. We dig trenches, care for children, type on computers. With our hands we draw plans for buildings, direct traffic, assemble cars. Some of us write math equations on chalkboards; others give trial evidence or perform in theaters. We give you thanks for all the ways we have been able to express ourselves through our work. We know that our labor contributes to society and connects us to others in our nation. Be with us as we work, encourage us when we are tired, help us appreciate the work others do, and keep our eyes on the higher goal of serving you in all the work that we do. In your name we pray, amen.

September 2

The big yellow buses are out and about now, Father. Children are making their way to school. Thank you for the opportunity that each one has to learn. Thank you for this country's dedication to public education, for the teachers and staff who work hard to make it happen.

The United States boasts great doctors, scientists, scholars, entrepreneurs, writers, researchers, actors, musicians, artists, technicians, athletes, and professionals in every field. Many of these folks started their educational odyssey when they boarded a school bus. So bless these children I see around me, Lord, as they learn and grow and find their own significant place in this big world. Bless the teachers who direct their learning. Bless this nation with a new generation of Americans who will lead the world in a positive direction.

September 3

All-loving God, sometimes I am overcome by the suffering in your creation. There are so many people in misery in our country and all over the world—those who have lost loved ones, those who are starving, cold, and hopeless. I know that everything happens for a reason, but those reasons are often impossible for me to understand. Help me trust you with everything, God. I need your peace that passes understanding today and every day. Amen.

★　★　★　★　☆

Just when all seems hopeless, prayer lifts us like a wave on the ocean. A sturdy craft, prayer doesn't hide from pain but uses it like the force of the sea to move us to a new place of insight, patience, courage, and sympathy. Always, it is God's hand beneath the surface holding us up.

September 4

Creator, we look to you for direction as we struggle with the choices placed before us. Help us make the right choice, to move forward with boldness and clarity of purpose as we try to right the wrongs we have been faced with. Provide us with guidance and patience as we unite in fellowship to protect our peace, our freedom. Creator, arm us with love, compassion, and common sense as we strive to claim our place in the world as the leaders of justice, hope, and liberty.

September 5

It's time to return to a fall schedule, to more industry and less play. But my work is a blessing from you, Lord. Through it I find purpose, I am a valuable part of a team, and I am able to make a living and provide for others. And, in a broader sense, I also help strengthen the fabric of this nation. So next time I get tangled up in the minutia of my daily tasks, God, remind me as an American to work in such a way that I can proudly stamp my efforts: "Made in the USA."

☆ ☆ ☆ ☆ ☆

Freedom isn't just a benefit of living in America. Freedom is America. It's in the metal, the pistons, the fabric of America. If we lose our freedom, we lose America.

September 6

For pastors, priests, rabbis, and other holy leaders, we give you praise. Thank you for the ways they encourage us, admonish us, and comfort us as ministers of grace. Thank you for the sacrifices they make and for the services they offer. We are a people blessed with noble, gracious servants who teach us how to love and how to give—not just with words but with their very lives. They marry us and bury us, and they touch our lives in sorrow and in joy. Be with them today, and give them what they so freely give to us. Amen.

☆ ☆ ☆ ☆ ☆

Open the gates, so that the righteous nation that keeps faith may enter in.

Isaiah 26:2

September 7

Dear Lord, help our country build a firm foundation by relying on your wisdom; by diligently seeking your direction in all we do; and by learning to walk in your path of kindness, peace, and justice.

We must always bear in mind the central purpose of our national life.... We work for a better life, so that men may put to good use the great gifts with which they have been endowed by their creator.

President Harry S. Truman,
State of the Union address, 1950

September 8

Take them up on angels' wings, the heroes who die for our freedom. Take them to the promised land, the workers who risk life and limb for our safety. Take them into your loving arms, the children who huddle in fear at night. Take them to the gates of heaven, the soldiers who fight for our causes. Take each man, woman, and child who suffers from adversity to a restful, peaceful place. Take the victims of violence to a land where only love exists. Take the wounded to a world where

there is no pain. Take them up on angels' wings, the heroes who once were our parents, our husbands or wives, our sons, our daughters, our friends.

September 9

Lord, in this land of plenty that we call home, give us wisdom to discern between necessity and surplus. Give us moderation as we acquire clothing, toys, and all the things we think we need. Show us the difference between needs and wants. Give us generous hearts that are willing to share with those who have less than we do and whose basic needs are not being met. Give us clear vision to see all the marvelous gifts you give each of us each day—sunshine, rain, air, natural beauty—so that we do not feel we must continually acquire more gifts of our own.

Help us maintain a clear distinction between what things we feel we deserve and what things we merely desire. In a land of plenty, help us identify a point of satisfaction and contentment so that we do not live each day merely for the sake of adding to what we already have. Amen.

September 10

We are blessed with a large country and a rich heritage. It is good to remember and consider all the good and gracious gifts we have received from your hand. Both your creations and ours are treasures worthy of preservation and praise.

Thank you, God, for museums, where these riches are stored. These institutions of learning help us keep in touch with our past and appreciate our talents, genius, bravery, and resourcefulness. Museums represent generations—past, present, and future. Thank you for them. Amen.

Smithsonian Institution, The Castle

September 11

Gracious and loving God, this day reminds us of life's fragility
and its strength;

> of unspeakable evil and unstoppable goodness;
> of how unrelated individuals can become a close-knit
>   community;
> of how brokenness can lead to wholeness.

On this day we learned what it is to be American.

Tragedy opened our hearts. We saw heroes and found them to
be ordinary people to whom we will be forever grateful. We
realized our shared nationality mattered more than any difference that divides us. We talked to neighbors, made friends,
spent time with loved ones, and prayed for peace.

When the intensity of this day faded, we may have fallen back
into old habits and forgotten our passion for life. May the

memory of this day spur us to appreciate the opportunity to live in freedom. Help us to live aware of our blessings. Bless those who grieve the losses of this day. Help us keep our eyes fixed on the peace that is possible only when we all work together in your spirit. Amen.

September 12

These are mean-spirited times, and we quake and shudder. Tend us, loving Creator, and shelter us in the palm of your hand against all that would uproot and destroy us. We are the flowers of your field.

☆ ☆ ☆ ☆ ☆

Tragedy often serves as a wake-up call to the heart, urging strangers to step away from themselves and move toward others. Neighbors who never knew each other suddenly realize that the world is much friendlier when they reach out in friendship.

September 13

You are everywhere, Lord, comforting and guiding us as we move through life's extremes. You are with us during births and deaths, in routine and surprise, in peace and conflict, and in stillness and activity. We cannot wander so far in any direction that you are not already there with us.

☆ ☆ ☆ ☆ ☆

Each prayer is a message of faith in God. We are saying, "I trust you; lead me. I believe in you; guide me. I need you; show me." When we offer ourselves openly, he will always answer.

September 14

Almighty God, you have blessed the United States with freedom of speech. We confess that we do not always think before we speak. Guard our tongues so we use this freedom wisely. Let us speak in love, not in anger. Let us speak of love, not of hate. Let us fulfill the expectations of our country's founders by letting love, along with freedom, ring from home to home, village to village, and shore to shore. In your name, amen.

★ ★ ★ ★ ☆

When we recognize the monumental gift of freedom, it is only then that we can truly appreciate its significance.

September 15

All powerful God,
we praise your name!
We see all you have done,
    and we want to dance and sing!
How great are your works!
When we want to take credit for our accomplishments,
    let us instead give glory to you.
When we try to control our lives,
    let us give our lives over to you.
When we are angry because things haven't turned out
    the way we planned,
help us to see the new way you have prepared for us.
When we don't want to be bothered with others' needs,
    fill us with your compassion.
All powerful God, we are your loving children.
Amen.

September 16

Sing out in celebration! Raise your voices to the heavens in gratitude and joy, for we are a strong and mighty people living in a strong and mighty nation! Sing for the cities that pulse with ideas and opportunities. Sing for the country where life bursts forth in bold colors. Sing for the prairies where the big sky reigns. Sing for the wheat fields, the corn fields, the thundering plains. Sing for the seashores, the beaches, and the lakes. Sing for the communities where people build homes and dreams. Sing for the neighborhoods where children laugh and play. Sing out, O America, sing loud and free and clear. We are a nation among nations. Let your voices ring out from sea to shining sea!

September 17

Your plan for our country, Lord, is that we follow those who uphold the right and the good. Your spirit fills those who walk in humility, patience, and self-sacrifice. Please open our eyes that we may see those gentle faces beckoning us upward and onward in a spirit of love. They are all around us, we're certain. Open our eyes!

☆ ☆ ☆ ☆ ☆

Let's revive the custom of blessing. When we bless someone, we show love and respect, encourage greatness and pride. Sincerely honoring the people and things in our lives is a wonderful way of showing gratitude to the Lord. Let's join God in blessing America.

September 18

Lord, when we have nothing left to hold onto, you provide us with hope as an anchor for our souls. Americans, and people throughout the world, need that hope now, and we pray that you will fill every broken place in our hearts with its reassuring light. Thank you, Lord, for in you we have an unending supply of hope in the midst of uncertainty and failure. We know that if we could see this situation through your eyes, we would see how you will bring us through it. We place our hope in you and you only. Amen.

September 19

Enliven my imagination, God of new life, so that I can see through today's troubles to coming newness. Surround me and my nation with your caring so that I can live as if the new has already begun.

☆ ☆ ☆ ☆ ☆

Each American citizen holds a piece of the puzzle that is our nation, since no one perspective or form of patriotism represents the whole. When we all join together with united hearts, the puzzle is complete. This wide array of ideas and impressions, this mixture of religions, ethnicities, and cultures: This is America.

September 20

Father,
Today, bless those who are teaching our children.
Bless them for
    their patience, their creativity,
    their devotion, their kindness,
    their commitment, their energy,
    their humility, their persistence,
    their smiles, their compassion,
    their wisdom, their knowledge,
    their friendliness, their vision,
    their courage, their responsibility.
And bless them for being so much more than teachers—bless
them for being friends, counselors, caring adults, guides, lis-
teners, and firm believers in the value of every young life. Bless
them, Father, a hundredfold.

September 21

God, your grace is our country's comfort in times of trouble
and our beacon of hope amid the blackness of despair. By
opening ourselves to your ever-present grace, dear God, we
know we are loved and cared for, and our hearts sing out in
joyful gratitude. Amen.

☆ ☆ ☆ ☆ ☆

One flag, one land, one heart, one hand,
One Nation, evermore!

Oliver Wendell Homes, Sr.,
"Voyage of the Good Ship Union"

September 22

Thank you, God, for the people you have chosen to be my family, my friends, and my fellow citizens. They are my guides, my teachers, my angels, and my cheerleaders. Though I may often be in conflict with them and we fight and argue and say things we regret, I am blessed to have these people walking beside me along life's path, helping me to grow and become who you created me to be. Amen.

★ ★ ★ ★ ☆

We trust in the Lord to care for us, and he, in turn, trusts in us to care for each other. We can honor his faith in us by pledging to serve our communities. We can truly live his love by caring for our neighbors.

September 23

Like autumn leaves we sometimes feel dry, uninspired, empty.
We feel exposed, unprotected—as individuals and as a nation.
Remind us that we are always in your care.
Your loving kindness is without end.
No matter how alone or empty we feel,
    you wrap us in your loving arms and hold us close.
In all seasons you are with us.
We are your beloved children.
Loving Parent, comfort and sustain us always. Amen.

September 24

God, our freedoms are much like the air we breathe; they are taken for granted until they are taken away. So today I pause to thank you for the freedoms our citizens have been able to enjoy: being able to freely worship, choosing what we will wear, voting for whomever we wish, deciding whether and whom we will marry, and having the freedom to travel from place to place.

This is just the beginning of a very long list. God, you are the author of freedom, the champion of the privilege to make one's own choices. Help us honor you today by choosing well and wisely.

September 25

Father God, as I watch the leaves begin to turn crisp and cover my yard with patches of gold, I know that nature knows just what to do. Through your grace, we, too, can trust your plan for us. I am just one believer, sitting alone and thinking about leaves and trust. But I know that, in spirit, I am not alone. The coins in my pocket speak for a nation. Their value in metal is negligible, but their message is profound. Every single one proclaims "In God We Trust." Thank you, God, for golden leaves and copper pennies of priceless encouragement. Amen.

★ ★ ★ ★ ☆

The thing that struck me most all over the United States was the physical beauty of the country, and the great beauty of the cities.

Gertrude Stein, *Everybody's Autobiography*

September 26

O Lord, hear my prayer for all who are in trouble this day.

Comfort those who are facing the loss of a loved one.

Encourage those who are finding it difficult to believe in the future.

Heal those who are suffering.

Uphold those who are being tempted in any way today.

In all these things, I ask your blessing. Amen.

September 27

Lord, there's a big old harvest moon hanging low in the sky, and the stars look so close you could reach out, grab a fistful, and touch heaven for a while.

They're bringing home the harvest, Lord. And soon, as if at some secret command, the leaves will turn to gold then red, fall in the chill wind, and hide the bareness of the fields until spring.

But tonight the sky is halo-bright, lit by a sacred lamp, a gateway to the stars. You feel so near on nights like this. We feel so close to others, too, knowing the same moon is lighting up all of America. Tonight, it's all one sky, one God, one people, all giving thanks as we gather in our harvest.

September 28

Thank you, Lord, for hot, fresh apple pie. Sure, I know it is a bit of a cliché. But it smells good, and it reminds me of a cool crisp autumn day. Why is it American? I'm not sure. But it is comfortable, warm, and safe, like home, or like when I've been overseas and step back onto the  soil of a land both safe and free. And apple pie warms me from the inside out, like mother's love. And your love. So thank you, God, for apple pie and for all the good things that remind me of home. Amen.

September 29

Source of all life and love, let this nation be
a place of goodness and opportunity,
a haven for those who are lonely,
a sanctuary of peace in the midst of the storm.
Above all, let us reflect the kindness
of your own heart, day by day.

☆　☆　☆　☆　☆

*What does it take to live a life of hope? Nothing more
than a willing heart.*

September 30

When autumn winds blow,
the handiwork of the
Lord becomes evident in
the glorious reds and
golds of leaves turning
colors and in the cool
evening breezes that bring

peaceful slumber. When autumn winds blow, the blessings of
the Lord become visible as Americans admire the pumpkin-
orange harvest moon hanging low over the horizon, which
reminds us that we will soon be celebrating Thanksgiving with
family and friends. When autumn winds blow, God looks
down upon these United States and sends warm kisses and
comforting hugs to be stored up for the cold winter to come.

October 1

I asked God, "What can one man do? What can one woman say? What can one child create that would possibly make a difference in a world of billions of people?"

God answered, "One man can pray. One woman can hope. One child can dream. One man can build. One woman can work. One child can play. One man can speak. One woman can organize. One child can share. One man can walk. One woman can march. One child can stand. One man can vote. One woman can write. One child can read. One man can teach. One woman can understand. One child can learn. One man can serve. One woman can love. One child can laugh. And that is all that need be done."

October 2

Every day I wake with trivial problems on my mind, Lord. I'm late for work, I didn't wash the kitchen floor yesterday, the house needs to be painted, and my bills are piling up endlessly. Lord, please help me to enjoy life's most precious gifts: my family, my health, and my freedom. Teach me to appreciate that which is around me and not to ache for things I don't have.

★ ★ ★ ★ ☆

I shall know but one country.
The ends I aim at shall be my country's, my God's, and Truth's.
I was born an American; I will live an American;
I shall die an American.

Daniel Webster

October 3

Autumn speaks of dying and decay, of a winding down of the cycle of life. Yet autumn has a beauty all its own, Lord, as greens are replaced by scarlets and golds and browns in rich profusion.

You have chosen this season to remind us that the closing of one door means the opening of another. Endings come, but they hold the promise of restoration.

You lead us through the seasons of our lives, Father, and give us beauty in each one. Autumn tells us there is still time to serve you, still much to give. Our hearts overflow with thankfulness for the bounty of our lives and the opportunities to live in the light of your love.

October 4

Father, in a nation that is filled
with different people, different
ideals, different beliefs, and
different goals, teach us to love.
Help us see others through your
eyes. Help us learn from others.
Help us listen to others. Help us
respect others. Help us honor
others. Help us encourage others.
Help us reach out to others. Help

us share with others. Help us applaud others. Help us rejoice
with others. Help us mourn with others. Help us join with
others so that, in this nation, there will no longer be
"others"—there will only be "us." Amen.

October 5

God, we are here on earth with a purpose: to do your will in whatever way we can in our daily life and work.

Our ancestors came to America filled with purpose. They came with the will to do what was needed to make our country prosper, to make America great and pleasing to your eyes. They worked hard and unfailingly. With each turn of the spade, each mile of prairie, and each prayer, our ancestors turned America into the great and prosperous country we live in today.

Help us add to this greatness. However humble our tasks, let us do our daily work with you, Lord, and with our country always in mind. Fill us with purpose, and grant us knowledge of your will for us and our glorious land. Let our children and grand-children state proudly that we, too, did God's work for the good of all America.

October 6

Today, God, I am appreciative of the gift of life. Thank you for blessing me with the love of family, friends, and neighbors. Thank you for giving me the freedoms of life, liberty, and choice. I take today as your most precious gift to live as a free American. Amen.

☆ ☆ ☆ ☆ ☆

Being an American means exercising great freedoms with an even greater grace.

October 7

So many times we take for granted the beauty of the land you have given us. Let us learn to honor the ground we walk upon, to praise the air we breathe and the water we drink. Let us live each day in gratitude for the abundant foods we eat and the sun that warms our bodies. Remind us of the awesome glory of a snow-capped mountain range and the wild, unencumbered spirit of a stormy shore. Let us never forget the magic of a prairie moon or the wonder of a starry desert sky. Let no sunset slip past our vision, let no amazing creature lack for our attention. Make us aware, dear Creator, of all that you have created for us, and teach us to care for it well.

October 8

Father, it hurts me to watch people in this country pull away from you, especially in times like these. We need you, Lord. We need your strength, courage, and hope. We need your help and direction and peace. I don't understand why the people who need you most acknowledge you least.

Please, Father, turn the hearts of your children back to you. Please help our people see how much you love them and how deeply you long to comfort and provide for them. Please make us strong by making us more dependent on you than ever before. Thank you, Lord, that you are always faithful even when we are not.

October 9

I will sing of your steadfast love forever!
I will proclaim your faithfulness to all generations!
For you are my God.
You love me beyond comprehension,
    and your hand steadies me lest I fall.
So I will stand to my full height and shout my praises.
There is none like God, maker of heaven and earth!

★ ★ ★ ★ ★

I hear America singing, the varied carols I hear.

Walt Whitman, "I Hear America Singing"

October 10

We are thankful for your angels, mighty warriors that come to us at your command. They comfort us, protect us, and carry us into your arms. You are Jehovah, the Lord of Hosts, and for this we give you praise.

I ask you to be Lord over the U.S. Army, too. Like your mighty angels, may our soldiers stand against the darkness, comfort the innocent, and protect us all with wisdom and skill. Give them courage and compassion, and use them to do your will. If in doing so they sacrifice their lives for the noble and the good, send your own angelic hosts to gather them into your arms. And give them peace. Amen.

October 11

Dear God, we're a nation of many peoples, ethnic backgrounds, beliefs, interests, and priorities. But, lately, Lord, I've sensed a new unity. We've remembered what it means to us—to all of us—to be Americans. We've been flying the flag, supporting our leaders, and thanking you for this great land.

Help us to maintain that oneness, Father. Help us to keep being grateful for our freedom and for one another. We pray that it won't take a crisis to inspire our patriotism.

☆ ☆ ☆ ☆ ☆

Let us at all times remember that all American citizens are brothers of a common country, and should dwell together in the bonds of fraternal feeling.

President Abraham Lincoln

October 12

United we stand, God, under your guard. Together, as neighbors and children of God, we can overcome any obstacle: hunger, war, hatred, and even fear. We look to you for guidance, approval, and love. With you as our leader, God, our nation stands strong. Amen.

☆ ☆ ☆ ☆ ☆

Let every nation know, whether it wishes us well or ill, that we shall pay any price, bear any burden, meet any hardship, support any friend, oppose any foe to assure the survival and the success of liberty.

President John F. Kennedy, Inaugural Address,
January 20, 1961

October 13

I thank you, Lord, for purple mountain majesties and for all the beauty that fills our land. I'm especially glad for fruited plains and all the good, and brotherhood, from sea to shining sea.

Help me see today all that you have made in a new way. Help me find my strength and joy in you. Amen.

★ ★ ★ ★ ☆

I lift up my eyes to the hills—from where will my help come? My help comes from the Lord, who made heaven and earth.

Psalm 121:1–2

October 14

Giver of Life, you created me and have loved me all my days.
Help me to remember that each day is a gift from you,
and let me so serve you that my life might be a blessing to
others.
Be in me, inspire me to acts of love, and let others know you
as they see me.
In thanksgiving for each day that I live and can serve, amen.

★   ★   ★   ★   ☆

*Not all medals of honor are pinned to shirts; some are inscribed
on souls, visible to God alone.*

October 15

Father, on this new day, be with the men and women who govern our nation. Give them wisdom as they make decisions. Give them discernment as they debate issues. Give them integrity as they deal with one another. Give them honesty as they deal with the public. Give them courage as they deal with other nations. The burdens and responsibilities they bear are greater than we realize. We are quick to criticize them and slow to thank them. But their role in our lives is critical as they

preserve a citizen-centered government. Bless and guide them as they serve the people of America. Amen.

U.S. Capitol building

October 16

God, you have given us another bright new morning. As we step out into this day, help us see it as a fresh chance to do your will. Let your love shine through us. Fill our thoughts with your divine wisdom. Fill our words with your compassion, and make our actions express your love. Help us do the best we can for the good of our families, our friends, and our country.

☆ ☆ ☆ ☆ ☆

America lives in the heart of every man everywhere who wishes to find a region where he will be free to work out his destiny as he chooses.

President Woodrow Wilson

October 17

Lord God, I remember today all my fellow Americans who are homeless, jobless, friendless, or experiencing some other kind of painful loss or struggle. I pray that you will guide them to the kind of help they need. Thank you for the many religious institutions, agencies, and programs that exist in this nation to give a helping hand. Please grant them the resources and wisdom to operate effectively. Last but not least, Father, open my own eyes to the needs all around me. I want to help heal the wounds of those in my country whose lives have been touched by personal hardship. In your name, amen.

☆ ☆ ☆ ☆ ☆

The beauty of creation inspires me to live a life where I, too, can create something beautiful.

October 18

Heavenly Father, this morning I rejoice in each infant born in every state across our land. I thank you that these little ones are born in freedom and not to weary mothers fleeing famine, wars, and persecution. I thank you that these children are born into a land of plenty, a nation that will educate them. I ask you to protect them, guide them, and help each one to use their

gifts for your glory and for the betterment of all humankind. Thank you, God, that our nation is committed to welcoming every child with equality, and, dear God, help me do my part to keep it that way. Amen.

October 19

God, I thank you for the rich heritage you've given America. In less than 300 years, Father, you've already blessed us with wise ancestors, great victories in war, and a history worth celebrating. You've also given each of us a personal American heritage. Our parents and their parents lived through that history and have now handed us the responsibility to continue the work of making America great and keeping her free.

Help us honor that heritage, Lord, by honoring their memories. Help us celebrate the blessings you've shown us. Help us seek your face as new challenges arise. And help us each do our part to build on the heritage of our ancestors so our children can be proud as well.

October 20

Lord, give us faith to carry on when the skies
   grow dark with fear.
Lord, give us hope to keep moving toward the light
   when the fog of ignorance grows thick.
Lord, give us compassion when we feel untrusting
   of others we meet along the way.
Lord, give us love when it seems as though
   hatred rules the day.
Lord, give us healing that we may one day know joy again.

★　★　★　★　★

*There is no problem too tough, no obstacle too great, that
America cannot overcome it—with God's help.*

October 21

For freedom of the press, we thank you, Lord. For the right to read a newspaper and write a letter to the editor, we give you praise.

We take it for granted, sometimes: the endless shelves of magazines, the hundreds of cable channels, the libraries filled with books free for the borrowing. But so many nations do not have this ocean of ideas. And so many people are not allowed to disagree with their own governments.

So we are glad. Help us to protect this freedom. And remind us to take advantage of it. Amen.

October 22

Blessed Lord, I heard a Chinese Christian prayer that says, "O Lord, reform our world, beginning with me." Help me remember that I must act instead of complain, give much rather than give in, offer my time, energy, and money rather than be stingy toward your people and my country. Remind me every time I feel hopeless and powerless that a single change begins one step at a time and that change begins with me. For your glory, amen.

☆ ☆ ☆ ☆ ☆

The greatness of our nation will not be measured by our gross national product or military power but by the compassion with which we respond to human needs at home and around the globe.

October 23

Heavenly Father, this harvest season I see once again the bounty of our land being gathered and stored so that America's winter is not a season of hunger. I thank you for each farmer and farm worker and ask you to bless all those who sow and reap. I thank you for the grocers who make this bounty available. I pray that our hearts may be bountiful, too, that we may share with those who hunger. I pray that our hearts grow large enough to ensure that not a single child weeps with hunger through cold and snowy nights.

October 24
United Nations Day

Since you formed us all as your children, O God, and not as separate nationalities, you must have been pleased when we came together as nations united. Help us to see ourselves as one whole, not many parts. Let the United Nations be a living symbol of your unity, of our kinship as human beings, of cooperation for the good of all people. Prevent us from making distinctions between rich and poor, powerful and humble, at war or at peace.

Hold before us the vision of one world, one people; give strength to those in the United Nations who work to bring about that vision. Guide them as they deal with war and rumors of war. Help those leaders hear the many voices of the international community as one voice; help them work as one body for peace with justice in all parts of the world. Amen.

United Nations building

October 25

I dreamt last night that hate was defeated and
    love ruled the earth.
I dreamt last night that hunger was wiped out and
    nourishment filled our bellies.
I dreamt last night that homelessness disappeared and
    shelter covered the land.
I dreamt last night that injustice was overcome and
    goodness filled all hearts.
I dreamt last night that despair was no more and
    hope shone eternal.
I dreamt last night that war ceased to be and
    peace settled on the land.
Some people say that dreams are for children.
I say that dreamers keep us alive.

October 26

The roots of our nation are drawn from all the countries of the globe. Our land was shaped by the best the world could offer. Americans come from everywhere, and every one of us carries within our hearts and souls a memory of some other place, passed on from generation to generation. How can we not feel one with the whole world?

Lord, you understand us when we pray for peace on earth and goodwill among all people. Help all of us, everywhere, make peace with ourselves and each other. Help all of us, everywhere, overcome our struggles, confusion, and misunderstandings. Join us in love and friendship with our brothers and sisters from all continents so that we truly may be one world under one God, united in your name.

October 27

God, you who created the heavens and earth and all things therein, we turn to you now and ask for your merciful love. Create in us all a new spirit of understanding as we struggle to come to grips with the world we live in. Create in us a will that cannot be broken no matter how deeply our mourning dares to bring us down. Create in us the promise of a happier tomorrow that we will one day rise with the sun and feel joy again. Thank you.

★ ★ ★ ★ ☆

America without God wouldn't be America. We're rooted in him, watered in him, and pruned by him. Without him we can't grow.

October 28

Heavenly Father, at dawn my heart is quiet beneath your hand, but soon I must step into our broken world. Give me the grace to see what I can mend. Perhaps a few kind words to a weary

soul will restore needed energy to someone strug- gling. Perhaps a kindly act of mine will be passed on to one who feels forgotten. Through you I know each act of love is a sword that

tears the fabric of evil. I do not need to know that I have made a difference. But surely I need to know that you are near, reminding me to look, to listen, and to obey. Amen.

October 29

Lord, we live in spiritual abundance. Help us share a little of our bounty with those who may need some. Keep us from harm so we can help our children feel safe. Grant us understanding so we can better help others cope with life's challenges. Send us healing so we can help our friends heal. Bestow upon us the gift of peace so we can carry it out into our world. Fill us with your spiritual gifts, and grant us the pleasure of sharing.

★ ★ ★ ★ ☆

America is a land of wonders, in which everything is in constant motion and every change seems an improvement.

Alexis de Tocqueville, *Democracy in America*

October 30

God, I want to thank you for the courage and patriotism of the men and women who have served this country in the military. Without their skills, without their sacrifices, without their deaths, we might very well have lost the freedoms that make

America great. Without these heroes, the United States would be a very different country today.

I praise you, God, for raising up men and women of courage to fight our battles in desperate times and to maintain our defenses in peaceful times. I praise you for working through those people to protect and defend us from enemies of every kind. Help us remember them and honor their sacrifices for us.

October 31
Halloween

Fall has come to America, Lord. Barn parties, fall festivals, hayrides, and, of course, trick-or-treaters—all are traditions of our country's communities, of our nation's neighborhoods.

However we choose to honor or celebrate our harvest, let us not forget to honor and celebrate you. Not a flower blooms nor a plant bears fruit without your touch. You have authored our freedom, blessed our way of life, and increased our harvest. Fall has come because you ordained it.

So thank you, God, for the parties and festivals and hayrides. For the ghosts and goblins. For the pumpkins, real and costumed. For the crisp air, the crunchy leaves, and the bulky sweaters. For all your good works. For your love and care. Amen.

November 1

God, our lives pour out from your spirit and flow like rivers into the ocean of life. At times we trickle along, swirling merrily over the stones scattered in our path. Sometimes we flow fast and smooth along a pleasant, narrow course, glistening and bubbling in the sun. In the rapids, our lives churn and tumble as we crash into rocks in unexpected places. But it's life, God, it's life, and we carry on with your guidance, trusting that we'll safely reach the ocean of your love.

Whatever lies in our course, help us flow over and around it. Help us keep moving, trusting, journeying, believing. In God we trust.

November 2

Father God, please look after all your children. Help us to forgo our gripes and grumbles with other Americans. Help us stand united not just at difficult times but at all times. We are a great nation; bigotry can only lead us to weakness. Amen.

★ ★ ★ ★ ★

When we reach out in love to all Americans, we demonstrate, in the most profound and significant way, our love for America.

November 3

The world around us is becoming cold. Temperatures are dropping. Frost often frames the windows, and snow will begin to cover the ground like a white blanket. God, although the outside is cold, please help us, as people, not to become cold. Let us not turn our backs on one another during hardships but, instead, hold out our hands in support. Please, God, let us know the joys of the crisp, cool air without knowing the anguish of being cold, hungry, and alone. Amen.

☆ ☆ ☆ ☆ ☆

When we awaken the sleeping lion of potential within, we allow it to spring forth in our lives with a mighty, joyful roar.

November 4

Thank you, Lord, for pilgrims who bravely sailed the treacherous seas to find a shore where they could worship you in freedom. Lord, create in me a pilgrim soul, determined, single-minded, and unafraid to stand in solidarity with good citizens whose ways are not my ways. Help me to love them, to learn from them, and to be ever mindful that our pilgrims' sacrifices created freedom for all, not just for me. Amen.

☆ ☆ ☆ ☆ ☆

Remember, remember always that all of us, and you and I especially, are descended from immigrants and revolutionists.

President Franklin D. Roosevelt, in a speech before the Daughters of the American Revolution, April 21, 1938

November 5

God, though we are grown, there are days when, more than anything else, we need a mommy to comfort us, protect us, hold us, and love us. The news is depressing. The economic outlook is gray. The job prospects are grim. The international scene is turbulent. It seems that, at any moment, things could take a turn for the worse and our lives could turn upside down, out of control. In those times, help us remember that you are there for us, ready to comfort, protect, hold, and love us— ready to mother anyone who calls out to you. Thank you for being a loving mother to our nation and for being a nurturing mother to each of us as individuals. Amen.

November 6

Glory to God in his heaven, for he has blessed us here on earth with gifts of plenty! Praise him for the freedoms we hold dear to our hearts, and give him joyful thanks for the pleasures of living in a land so beautiful. Worship and adore him for creating such a strong and united nation where people of all faiths, colors, and creeds can stand together hand in hand. Thank you, God, for this land of dreams achieved, hopes fulfilled, and glories manifested.

☆ ☆ ☆ ☆ ☆

America. . . . It is a fabulous country, the only fabulous country;
it is the only place where miracles not only happen,
but where they happen all the time.

Thomas Wolfe, *Of Time and the River*

November 7

Thank you, Lord, for steeples. Thank you for the many churches, synagogues, and mosques and the many people and faiths they represent. Thank you that they point toward heaven and toward you.

Our nation is richly blessed with reminders that we should look to you. Our motto is "In God We Trust." But it's not just a motto, it's a motivation and a method—a way of looking at our past and to our future.

So give our pastors, rabbis, imams, priests, and elders wisdom. Guard their hearts, and deliver them from temptation. Help them each week to point us to that which is noble and true. But help them most of all to point us to your throne and, ultimately, to you. Amen.

November 8

Merciful Father, through our country's best and worst days, teach us to pray and help us make prayer a priority in our land.

Prayer is an act of love, uniting us with each other and with you. Loving God, you shape the world by prayer. Each time we honor you by seeking your presence, we become dif-  ferent people. Our attitude changes, our vision expands, and our country becomes richer.

Rule over our lives, O God. Heal our brokenness, and make us a nation of prayer once again. Thy will be done.

November 9

Heavenly Father, thank you for music that reminds me who I am and why I am here. Birds cheer me, and their songs remind me to scatter seeds. Sacred music reminds me that I am your child and that I must constantly look to you for guidance.

America's patriotic songs tell me that I live in the land of the free and that this citizenship carries responsibility.

Thank you, God, for your gift of music. Thank you for all the reminders that music invokes. Amen.

November 10

Dearest God, in his psalms David praised you because he was fearfully and wonderfully crafted by you in his mother's womb. Now, Mother God, I praise you for so carefully and wisely crafting this nation from its infancy. From the first, your hand of blessing was on the people who sought your guidance as they wrote our documents and set our course.

Thank you for birthing us when and how you did. As we continue to grow, God, help us grow in you. Please give our leaders the same wisdom, the same commitment to freedom and democracy. Please give them the courage to stand against those who would steal that freedom. Help us grow as we were born—in you.

November 11
Veterans Day

I want to remember the veterans of foreign wars today, dear
Lord. Many still live among us, some suffering silently from
wounds of body, soul, and spirit. I ask that you would heal
them by your consoling Spirit; free them from the turmoil of
heart and mind that would keep them from enjoying the very
liberties for which they fought.

The sacrifice of our veterans is moving and humbling, Father,
in light of my life of relative ease and safety. I pause this
moment to honor these brave men and women, bowing my
head in reverence and gratitude for their selfless and heroic
efforts to preserve life and liberty for others. Bless our veterans, dearest God! In your merciful name, amen.

Arlington Cemetary

November 12

Great Spirit, today we give
thanks for the harvest of blessings you have given us. For the
beauty of the natural landscape
and the diversity of wildlife,
thank you, Spirit. For the prosperity and opportunity this
nation provides us, thank you,
Spirit. For the freedom to
express ourselves as individuals,
thank you, Spirit. For the strength and courage of our leadership, thank you, Spirit. For the liberties we so often take for
granted, thank you, Spirit. Our hearts overflow with gratitude
and praise.

November 13

We thank you, Lord, for the freedoms we enjoy and for the good land you have given us. Thank you for America's compassionate people, who serve willingly and heroically in times of stress.

We have been blessed far beyond what we could ever think or imagine—far beyond what we deserve. Yet, we ask for your continued shower of blessings upon our country as we face the unknown.

Guide us, Father, and teach us how to live gracefully in a society filled with uncertainty. Help us to comfort one another and to show the world we are still your people.

November 14

Eternal God, it is hard to grasp that we live in eternity today. We do what we need to accomplish, we plan ahead as much as we are able, but we can never view the future in its fullness. Will our struggles for justice bring a new tomorrow? Do any of our actions ultimately make a difference? Give us the courage to act and the faith to believe that if we act with goodness in our hearts, and with your help, a new future can be born. You have been with us since the beginning and will be with us past the end; please fill our hearts this day, and help us live in your eternity. Amen.

☆ ☆ ☆ ☆ ☆

Faith delivers us from sad yesterdays and sends us toward happy tomorrows.

November 15

Prepare my heart, O God, for this season of Thanksgiving. I have so much to be grateful for as a citizen of the United States. Regardless of my race, religion, or gender, I have a voice, a vote, and validity as a person of intrinsic worth. My rights are protected by the law, and a system of checks and balances helps prevent corruption in seats of power that might threaten those rights. I praise you, Lord, for my rights and privileges, and I thank you that they are upheld by a nation whose code of ethics gives dignity to its citizens.

☆ ☆ ☆ ☆ ☆

Freedom and independence are two of life's most precious gifts.

November 16

Father, the headlines often do little to encourage and uplift us as a nation. The things that are reported are often the worst of the worst. Bad news seems to be the most popular news. But we need to hear the good news. For every crime, we know that there are a thousand acts of kindness. For every act of dishonesty, we know that there are a thousand acts of goodness. For every lie that is told, we know that there are a thousand encouraging words spoken. God, help us see and recognize the things all around us that will never make the headlines but that are the most newsworthy of all. Amen.

November 17

During this time of thanks, I want to go one step beyond "thank you for my family and thank you for this food." Thank you, God, for my country, my family of Americans, and, most importantly, my freedom. May you continue to watch over this country and guide its leaders to make informed decisions about its future. May our country continue to be the home of the free and the brave. Amen.

☆ ☆ ☆ ☆ ☆

In order to stand strong and survive, a nation must be built on a solid foundation of unchanging truth.

November 18

Forgive us our debts. We owe so much to so many.

Today, Lord, help me to thank someone who serves me, my community, and my country. There is a firefighter who needs to be encouraged and a police officer who needs a smile. There is a teacher who needs a flower and a pastor who needs a prayer. There is a crossing guard who needs a wave and a garbage collector who needs a handshake.

So forgive us our debts, as we try to pay them back. Amen.

☆ ☆ ☆ ☆ ☆

I like the Americans because they are healthy and optimistic.

Franz Kafka, author

November 19

Thank you, God, for libraries. Thank you for quiet places tucked into the corners of our neighborhoods and schools and homes filled with the ideas and imagination of the ages. It is good to be blessed with the wisdom of the past and visions of tomorrow. We thank you for

classics and for criticism, for poetry and for praise, for novels and for nonsense—for the rich cacophony of words that fills our hearts and minds with awesome, endless possibilities.

Give us now and always eager minds and hopeful hearts. And give us books. Amen.

November 20

Today we pray for and celebrate our older Americans. They are living proof of our country's history. During their lifetimes, they have gathered your wisdom and passed it on to the next

generation. They have given us examples of honesty, integrity, and hard work.

Protect our older citizens, Lord. As a nation, show us how best to care for these precious natural resources. Teach us to cherish those who have spent their lives helping to build up our great country.

November 21

In praise and thanksgiving, we stand before thee, O Lord. You have given us a harvest of plenty, a bounty of blessings no other nation can claim. Now teach us to share our overflowing cornucopia of good with others, Lord. Teach us how to give of our harvest and share the fruit of our fields so that the entire world can benefit from the wonderful riches we so proudly cultivate. Make us the gardeners of the world, tending to the needs of those who have so much less. Let us spread the seeds of love and caring and goodwill to all four corners of the globe, nurturing the growth of others so that life itself will bloom forth where there was only barren soil. Amen.

November 22

As winter arrives and we anticipate the coming holidays, I thank you, God, for the national mood of celebration and festivity that is shared by so many Americans. In this season of cheer and goodwill, place your Spirit of peace and love among us and within us.

Help us collectively to focus on the more meaningful aspects of the holidays, even as commercialism and stress attempt to push them out of our hearts and minds. Make us kinder toward one another as we look for parking places and shop, more willing to slow down and look out for the elderly and infirm among us, more patient with those who are working overtime to serve us during this busy season. And remind us to take time out to worship and thank you for the blessings of life, home, family, faith, and country. Amen.

November 23

Father, at this time of year, we talk a lot about giving thanks to you for all you've done for us as a nation. In that spirit, I wish to thank you for providing for those first families who made their homes on these shores. They came looking for freedom of religion and for opportunity. It wasn't easy for them, God, especially in the winters. Many died from disease and cold and hunger.

But you honored their sacrifice and faithfulness to you, as well as their desire to live as free people. You were with them through the long winters and as they grew and prospered. And you're still with us, their descendants. Thank you for your protection, provision, and hope. Help us be as faithful to you as they were, Lord.

November 24

Lord,

I may be one, but with others I become many.

I may be small, but with others I become mighty.

I may be weak, but with others I become strong.

I may be afraid, but with others I become courageous.

I may be weary, but with others I become energized.

I may be uncertain, but with others I become emboldened.

I may be confused, but with others I become clear.

I may be one, but with others I become many.

☆ ☆ ☆ ☆ ☆

Even when life seems perfect, our souls still need to be renewed.
Change keeps us fresh.

November 25

Make a joyful noise to the Lord, all the earth.
Worship the Lord with gladness;
come into his presence with singing.

Know that the Lord is God.
It is he that made us, and we are his;
we are his people, and the sheep of his pasture.

Enter his gates with thanksgiving,
and his courts with praise.
Give thanks to him, bless his name.

For the Lord is good;
his steadfast love endures forever,
and his faithfulness to all generations. Psalm 100

November 26

Loving Parent, thank you for all the families in our country. God, bless them richly. For those without a family, we ask you to bring people into their lives who can fill that role. For those with broken families, we ask you to bring comfort, healing, and hope for new beginnings. For those with traditional families, we ask you to bring energy and love to daily life. For those with nontraditional families, we ask you to bring acceptance and welcoming arms in the surrounding community. For those who have never known the joyous miracle of extended family—aunts, uncles, grandparents, cousins—we ask you to bring multitudes of people into their lives who can provide laughter, fun, encouragement, and a sense of belonging.

Thank you for the miracle of family. Keep our families strong, stable, and thriving. Amen.

November 27

Good and gracious Lord, you have been with us since the beginning, when a small, ragged band of pilgrims grew into a diverse nation of millions of people. You guided and strengthened our founders as they struggled to shape our great country.

Through the years, as we trusted you and clung to your promises, you have upheld us through the dark days and led us into the light.

We thank you for your faithfulness, Heavenly Father, and we ask you to continue to light the way for us as we face the future armed with the courage and compassion you have supplied.

November 28

Lord, be our guest.

You call us to your table and fill it with the bounty of your harvest. May the food we share nourish our bodies as your love nourishes our souls.

Bless the children at this table. They are born of the love you placed in our hearts. To them belongs the future. Help us guide them well. Show us how to sow the seeds of faith so they reap a harvest of peace and plenty in years to come.

Bless the parents, grandparents, and family at this table. Guide us so we can honor your name and live your word. Grant us the strength and insight to sow what we wish to reap and to prepare the fields of the future for our children.

Bless those we love who are not at this table today. Wherever in the world they are, let the love of this family fill their hearts until they come home again.

And, Lord, bless those we love who sit at your table instead of ours today. We are together in spirit until the day you call us home, when we can feast together in eternity. Lord, be our guest.

November 29

Dear God, I got to know my neighbor today. And what did I find out? That although he is of a different ancestry, he is just like me. That although he practices a different religion, he is just like me. That although he speaks a different language, wears different clothes, and eats different food, he is just like me. I got to know my neighbor today, and I found out that he, like me, is human.

★ ★ ★ ★ ☆

Tolerance is not about acknowledging people and accepting their beliefs; rather, it is just the opposite—accepting people and acknowledging their beliefs.

November 30

The sun rises on me each day, Lord, and I wake up in a place known the world over as the strongest nation on earth. In the course of a day, I don't usually think much about that fact, but

when I hear in the news about the struggles and instability in other parts of the world, I wonder sometimes what it must be like. Father, today I pray for all the people  who struggle to find justice and peace wherever they are. I ask that you will comfort those who are suffering and show me how I can help bring them relief. Keep the United States strong and free and willing to help secure liberty and justice for all. Amen.

December 1

God, the light has faded from the sky, and the first stars have begun to shine through a velvet night.

Those stars, Lord God, fill me with wonder. Each bright point is one among many and still a brilliant, shining sun in its own right. No matter how brightly they shine, they never blind each other's light. Maybe people could learn something from the stars. But didn't you tell us, Lord, that your words were written in the heavens?

☆　☆　☆　☆　☆

One loves America above all things, for her youth, her greenness, her plasticity, innocence, good intentions, friends, everything.

William James, in a letter to Mrs. Henry Whitman, 1899

December 2

Heavenly Father, help me set aside my personal fears and concerns and lift up our president, whose burdens are far greater than mine. Give him moments of family time when he can set aside the cares of a nation. Give him moments of joy in your creation—time to enjoy the song of a bird, the unfolding of a bud, the swaying of shadows on the grass, a tasty meal. Give him time, God, and let life's simple and refreshing pleasures renew his spirit. Amen.

The White House

December 3

Dear God, be our shelter from the turbulent storms that threaten to blow us about like feathers in the wind. Be the foundation that we build our house of hope upon. Comfort us when we are afraid and confused. Be the guiding light that helps us find our way back home to where our loved ones wait for us. And one day lead us into paradise to spend eternity with those we have loved and lost. Amen.

★ ★ ★ ★ ☆

It is part of the American character to consider nothing as desperate, to surmount every difficulty by resolution and contrivance.

President Thomas Jefferson, in a letter to Martha Jefferson, March 28, 1787

December 4

Heavenly Father, we confess that we have not always treated other countries with the respect due them. Out of ignorance, we have made enemies and created resentment. Forgive us, Lord, for our oversight.

In times of trouble, we have learned who our friends and enemies are. Help us nurture our friendships and make peace with our enemies.

Make us sensitive to the rights of people of other races and creeds. Help us understand and improve relationships with those who should be our allies. Help us give them the respect they deserve.

You number the hairs of our heads. You acknowledge the value of each individual. Lord, help us do the same.

December 5

God, as we leave our homes this morning and head to the
workplace, give us your spirit of kindness, love, humility, and
concern. As we come in contact with others, help us express
these things in a genuine way. Help us smile when it would be
easier to scowl. Help us encourage when it would be easier to
criticize. Help us sympathize when it would be easier to con-
demn. Help us display an attitude of love that is impossible to
feel on our own. We want to be people who stand out from the
crowd—not because of power or superiority—but because of
our interactions with others. We want to change the world—
not through control or dominance—but through kindness,
love, and gentleness. Help us, God, for these things we cannot
do on our own. Amen.

December 6

God, give us the fortitude
to bear the long, cold
winter days ahead. Keep
us in good health as the
stiff wind blows through
to our bones and the rains
pour down unceasingly.

Remind us all of the importance of this time of rest for ourselves and for our nation, a time to contemplate the death of
old ideas and worn-out ways, a time when the present lies
dormant and the future awaits us, full of possibilities. For
without the winter, without the time to retreat into ourselves,
our homes, and our hearts, we would not be ready to be born
anew in spring.

December 7

We are a nation made great by the sacrifices of many who worked hard and did the right thing. I want to be one of them. So lead me not into temptation, but deliver me from evil. Deliver me from selfishness and sin and from putting myself first. Please, dear God, deliver me from evil. Amen.

☆ ☆ ☆ ☆ ☆

The spirit of America lives in us all. We can all help make that spirit stronger if we just act on our values of truth, freedom, and justice and remember that together we are America.

December 8

Lord, we realize how much we love our families and how important our friends are. But help us, Lord, to understand that even those who are strangers to us deserve our love and concern. Teach us to reach beyond the boundaries of our homes, our neighborhoods, and our cities and to lend a helping hand to whoever reaches out to grasp it. Show us how to be good citizens, Lord, in good times and in bad. Amen.

☆ ☆ ☆ ☆ ☆

No one will remember anything you did, unless, of course, you were kind to them.

December 9

Creator God, the eagle is making a comeback! I believe that you delight in the stewardship of the watchful caretakers who have guarded the existence of this majestic bird. They have seen to it that our national symbol did not disappear from the face of the earth. Thank you, Father. Thank you for the people who have an interest in preserving forests, prairies, and oceans; bears, alligators, and pelicans; the Everglades, the Rockies, and the Great Lakes. Thank you that you have knit the American people together with our different interests, abilities, and passions to do our part to make this country strong, while preserving its special beauty. Help us as people who have vastly varied perspectives to understand and respect one another. Help us not to villainize those who differ from us but to acknowledge the validity of their concerns. Let the American eagle remind us that we can survive and thrive if we make the effort to do so.

December 10

Dear God, in the north, it's cold today. The thought of sunshine and green grass is a distant wish. Will summer ever come
again? And in the south, it's warm today. What a strange world
this is, when half of our country can be outdoors swimming
while the other half is bundled up in mittens, caps, and long
johns. Give those in the tundra a sense of warmth and peace
and hope. Give those in the desert a sense of relief and joy and
thankfulness. And give us all a sincere appreciation for the
place we inhabit, whatever the weather may be. Amen.

☆ ☆ ☆ ☆ ☆

*Offering hope to others through a loving word, a thoughtful act,
or a simple smile is the surest way to lift your own spirit.*

December 11

God, shed your grace upon this nation. The grace to see the abundance of blessings contained therein. The grace to appreciate the freedoms and liberties we enjoy. The grace to prosper and help others to prosper by doing the work we love. The grace to live our days as we please, to love as we please, to be what we please. Shed your grace upon us, dear God, as we strive to make our country all that we collectively dream it can be.

☆ ☆ ☆ ☆ ☆

These Americans believe that everything is possible.

Fredrika Bremer, *America of the Fifties*

December 12

Heavenly Father, today I remember that Theodore Roosevelt said it is better to dare mighty things, even if we fail, than to live in the gray twilight that knows neither victory nor defeat.

Lord, please reveal to me my twilight places where fear of defeat keeps me from daring to do important things. I could write a letter to an elected representative knowing that he or she may never read it—yet it might be the letter that turns a vote. I could join, or even start, a neighborhood group that works to reduce crime. Lord, so many good things that I could do have "failure" written all over them. But so did founding a nation without a king.

God, please shine your light in my twilight places, and give me courage to risk failure. Amen.

December 13

We are a nation of caring individuals. We help other countries in their times of need. We aid them during wars and reach our hands across the ocean in times of crisis. Never do we expect to see others return the favor. We are a giving nation. But we cannot sustain ourselves alone. We need your support, God. With that we can do anything. Amen.

☆ ☆ ☆ ☆ ☆

Compassion is the ability to walk in another's shoes, even if they are several sizes too small. Compassion is understanding another's challenges, even if they are not our own. Compassion is caring for the welfare of others, even if they are different from us.

December 14

Thank you, God, for the psalm of David that says: "This is the day that the Lord has made; let us rejoice and be glad in it." Keep me mindful every moment that your word does not say, "Today just happened, so muddle through it." Thank you that *this* day offers my family, my neighbors, my country, the whole world, and me something to celebrate and be glad about. Despite personal sorrows and cares, every person of faith can rejoice in your promise of eternal life; every American can rejoice in our birthright of justice and freedom; every human can rejoice in having a Heavenly Father who listens to their every word. Thank you, God, for *this* day. Amen.

December 15

Someone on my street needs you today, God. Perhaps they need me to act on your behalf. We are all carriers of grace, and our private, gracious acts give our country and communities their strength. So use me, God, to shine your light of radiance and love onto my street. Give me the eyes to see your will and give me the strength to do it. A neighbor needs someone to smile, or to bake a plate of cookies, or to pick up the kids after school. Lord, make me that someone. Amen.

December 16

In days of uncertainty, we become hesitant and afraid to lead
our normal lives: to spend money, to travel, to celebrate, to
laugh. But you have told us, Lord, to be of good cheer. You
have overcome the world and its woes. You have set your eyes
on our country, Father. We are your people, and you are our
mighty fortress. We trust in you; help us face the future without fear.

★　★　★　★　☆

When you see a shadow fall across our land,
trust in the light of God behind it.

December 17

With praise I come to you this morning, Lord, in thanksgiving for the certainties in our uncertain lives. I do not question that the sun will rise or that the tides will turn on schedule. I do not wonder if robins will announce each spring and falling leaves will warn us to prepare for a cold winter. I do not question that I will die and rise up in your radiant presence. I do not question our national pride, for I know that no matter how hard democracy is put to the test, someone will stand and wave our flag. Even if that flag is tattered, Americans will unite and rally. I thank you, God, that I am also certain of that. Amen.

December 18

Thank you, God, for work.

Thank you for the contribution I can make and for the rewards I receive for doing it. My reward is not just the check or even the satisfaction of doing my best. Sometimes my reward is a smile from a customer, a pat on the back from a supervisor, a curious question from a coworker. Everywhere, every day, across our nation people do their work with diligence and grace—we are a productive people made great through an accumulation of small contributions. I'm glad to offer one of them.

So today, God, give me work to do and joy in doing it. May one of the smiles I receive be yours. Amen.

December 19

Lord, winter is the time when all nature sleeps within the earth. You send the winds to howl around it, the sleet to fall on it, the frost to nip it, the ice to glaze over it, and the snow to cover it all up in sparkling splendor.

In many parts of our country, winter is a difficult time of year. But you help us see the beauty in this season. You help us enjoy the cozy warmth of our homes, seek the perfection in a flake of snow, inhale the crisp air, and taste the bite of winter with its promise of the spring to come.

In the winter of our lives, Lord, when we must receive more than we can ever give, help us look toward the hope of an eternal springtime with you.

December 20

Lord, you are the God of all peace. As Joshua observed, you are Jehovah Shalom, the Lord our peace. Yet there is trouble in the world today. There are conflicts and wars. There are divorce proceedings and custody disputes. There are family battles, political battles, and military battles. And still, where you are, there is peace. So be with me today, God, and calm my heart. But more than that, fill our nation with your presence and soothe our troubled souls. We need you. We need your peace. Amen.

★ ★ ★ ★ ☆

Hopeful eyes look upward, penetrating the thick blanket of clouds to the clear blue skies beyond.

December 21

Thank you that in the deep, dark winter there are holidays to brighten our lives. Thank you for family, for traditions, for the freedom in this nation to celebrate or to not celebrate the holy

days of all faiths. This freedom Americans have—to choose our faith, to choose our celebrations, to choose our traditions—reflects your

own gift of free will to each of us. Thank you that you never force or coerce us to love you, and yet you offer your love freely if we desire it. O Father, I praise you right now for the gifts of free will and a free country. In your name, amen.

December 22

Lord, there is a crystal chill in the wind that carries the
promise of snow to freeze the lakes and dust the mountains.
It whispers of swirls and fronds on ice-frosted windows, brittle
stems of grass and bracken in winter fields, sluggish streams
that crawl their way between the woodland pines.

It's time to rest, to step back and watch as the earth holds its
breath. Time to dream and wonder while snowflakes drift
lazily down to smooth the contours of the world.

Lord, in you we find warmth and shelter from the cold. Grant
us rest to renew our bodies, peace to renew our dreams, and
your blessing to smooth our path in the spring to come.

December 23

For the right to disagree, God, I thank you. For the right to peaceably disagree and to assemble, I give you praise.

Freedom is a difficult concept to explain or understand, but we have the Bill of Rights, which guarantees us freedom to worship and assemble and protest.

So thank you, God, for a government of laws designed to make us free. Make us wise stewards of these rights. May we use our freedom to care for others and to honor you. Amen.

☆ ☆ ☆ ☆ ☆

I love the Americans because they love liberty.
William Pitt, First Earl of Chatham, March 2, 1770

December 24
Christmas Eve

Thank you, Mother God, for the promise of Christmas—
peace on earth. We have had holiday decorations in the mall
for months, it seems. And we have been eagerly waiting for
Christmas. But the thing we need, as individuals and as a
nation, is your peace.

You've shown us the way to peace by sending your son as a gift
and as a sacrifice. Through this, our relationship with you can
be restored. Make us a people marked by the same sacrificial
love, a nation with a generosity and grace that renews relationships and restores peace.

As we do this, give us your peace. Amen.

December 25
Christmas Day

Father, thank you for the many houses of worship in our land. We are so blessed to be able to sing, pray, and gather together without fear of punishment or imprisonment. Be with those in other nations who cannot worship freely. Give them courage and perseverance. Help us be aware of their situation so we can continue to pray for them and never take our own religious freedom for granted. The fellowship we enjoy with other worshipers is foundational in our lives. Thank you for giving us a country that protects that fellowship. Amen.

December 26

Dear God, if I truly look, I see your face. I see you in the smile of the disabled woman who carefully bags my groceries. I see you in the crossing guards at my neighborhood school. I see you in the people putting coins in a jar labeled "Feed the Hungry" beside a cash register. I see you in our nation's legislators as they begin their ses-

sions with prayer. Lord, humans will always be found wanting, but let us all recognize that so many people across our land are truly trying to be cheerful, helpful, and responsive to your heavenly laws. Amen.

December 27

E pluribus unum. Out of many, one. Out of many states, one nation. Out of many individuals, one country.

Lord, we are not sure how this nation works, but we are thankful it does. Perhaps it works because we respect each other or because we need each other. Perhaps it works because we honor you. Whatever the reason, we stand united against our enemies. We don't just rally around the flag, we rally around each other. Thank you for helping us make it work. Amen.

☆ ☆ ☆ ☆ ☆

An American Religion: Work, play, study, live, laugh, and love.

Elbert Hubbard,
The Roycroft Dictionary and Book of Epigrams, 1923

December 28

Lord, you have showered your favor upon us daily. You have given us the privilege to live in a country where citizens can take an active part in government and civil rights are respected more than anywhere else on earth. We are grateful for the godly men and women, shaped by your love and listening to your word in their hearts, who make this vision of freedom work.

Teach us to be worthy of all that we receive. Make us truly thankful that we are citizens of a great nation. Grant us a strong faith, and help us to face the tasks ahead with our heads held high.

December 29

Lord, the old year is drawing to a close, and a new one is about to begin. Once again we stand at a threshold.

A threshold, Lord, is a place of change, where we have the chance to leave behind the things we no longer need and ready ourselves for the new. Every threshold is an invitation to cast off ballast and move ahead unburdened.

Help us, Lord, to gracefully release the burdens of the past and ask forgiveness where it is needed. Help us to carefully choose what to carry into the new year. Help us make plans that bring out the best in us and serve your purpose for our lives.

Walk with us across the threshold between the years, and show us how to greet the future eagerly and openly, knowing you will guide us in love through whatever lies ahead.

December 30

Father, forgive this nation
for any and all wrongs she
has committed against the
land, the environment,
and humanity. We are a
good and strong nation,
with much to be proud of,

but we are not perfect. We have made mistakes. We are sorry.
Help us learn from our mistakes, for if we do not, we will have
made yet another unfortunate mistake for which there is no
excuse. As we move forward, let us always keep an eye on our
past so that our errors are not repeated. Amen.

December 31

Tomorrow we begin a new year, God. I want to thank you for what I have achieved to this point. Help me look beyond what is wrong in my life and in this world and look forward to better days and times. Help me broaden my views and aim for goals that are not so easily reached. Strengthen my belief in myself, and please do the same for all the citizens of the United States. God, help me and other Americans look forward to this new year with hope. Amen.

★ ★ ★ ★ ☆

Remember the past, and learn from its mistakes.
Honor the present, and make each moment count.
Dream the future, and work hard to make the dream come true.

Give me your tired, your poor,
Your huddled masses yearning to breathe free,
The wretched refuse of your teeming shore.
Send these, the homeless, tempest-tossed, to me,
I lift my lamp beside the golden door!

Emma Lazarus, "The New Colossus,"
inscription on the Statue of Liberty